soulmates

soulmates

understanding the true gifts
of intense encounters

SUE MINNS

HODDER
MOBIUS

First published in Great Britain in 2004 by Hodder and Stoughton
A division of Hodder Headline
This paperback edition published in 2005

A Mobius Book

10 9 8 7 6 5 4 3 2 1

A CIP catalogue record for this title is available from the British Library

ISBN 0340 82731 9

Typeset in Sabon by
Palimpsest Book Production Limited, Polmont, Stirlingshire

Printed and bound by
Mackays of Chatham Ltd, Chatham, Kent

Hodder Headline's policy is to use papers that are natural, renewable
and recyclable products and made from wood grown in sustainable
forests. The logging and manufacturing processes are expected to
conform to the environmental regulations of the country of origin

Hodder and Stoughton Ltd
A division of Hodder Headline
338 Euston Road
London NW1 3BH

contents

For Nick, Joff and Rodney.
And the others, who will never know
how much they gave me.

Thank you.

introduction

Yes, this is another book about soulmates. And if you have picked it up in the hope that it is an instruction manual on how to find your soulmate, you may be disappointed. Unless, of course, you are prepared to find out more about what a soulmate *really* is.

If someone tells you that they have met this enigmatic creature called a soulmate, you might imagine that they have found another person, possibly of the opposite sex, with whom they can be themselves totally and unreservedly. There are no barriers between the two of them, no critical judgement, lots to talk about and a feeling that they have known this person for ages – which they certainly will have. Does everyone have such a complementary partner waiting for them in the wings? How do you know if this *is* your soulmate and, if it is, will it last for ever? These questions will be addressed during the chapters of this book, and will, hopefully, be irrelevant by the end of it. Idyllic partnerships do exist of course, but for most of us it has been more of a struggle than a fairytale romance.

Through the following pages it is my intention to open up the whole business of soulmates: why there is such current interest in them, whether there is only one or many for each of us, and to debunk some of the myths that surround them. Do we really all believe that there is that one person out there somewhere who will make life okay? And once we find them, that life will run on oiled wheels, everyday problems will become insignificant and we will feel as if we have found the missing piece of our life's jigsaw? This 'other' is supposed to be our complement physically, emotionally and spiritually. Taking away the pain of isolation, of being misunderstood, they will restore meaning to our lives. The name that has been designated to this person who will rescue us from the humdrum and reconnect us to a sense of being fully alive is 'soulmate', and this book is an attempt to explore the meaning behind, in front of and right through that word.

Perhaps our search for the 'ideal' partner – this soulmate – stems from the fact that there is a general sense that we have somehow lost our way, here on earth, that it's all too harsh and difficult and somewhere over the rainbow, skies are blue. In these hectic modern times, it seems as if we have lost our connection to living in the world as a whole and narrowed it down to an existence that is centred round our own personal worlds. Gone is the sense of sacredness in nature. Gone is the sense of trust in those who lead us. Gone is the feeling that we are all part of a whole and that a positive future awaits us. It can all seem pretty depressing. Perhaps the increasing interest in the soulmate subject is because we are all searching for peace and tranquillity, and the sense that we are not alone.

Or perhaps there are other reasons . . .

Fairytales: Fact or Fantasy?

Every culture in the world has its own brand of myth and legend, handed down through the generations to give a message about life which is encoded in the tale. These stories involve all the human qualities we are likely to need and encounter on our journey from birth to death. Here in the west we have fairy stories. We learn from these tales that one day a knight in shining armour, or a beautiful maiden will appear and all our troubles will be over. I don't think anyone could really subscribe to that view in these pressurised times, but perhaps all of us carry the seed deep within us that it will be all right in the end. This part of the myth is true. But the happily ever after part cannot be delivered by anyone with two legs until we fully understand the dynamics at work within ourselves.

If we take a closer look at fairytales, we see that every one worth telling has elements of trial and tribulation, of danger and difficulty, before the princess awakes, the prize is won and everyone walks off into the sunset holding hands. But there's no value to a prize won without some kind of effort. It is my sincere belief that a soulmate encounter *may* feel like arriving at an oasis on a journey through the desert, but more often than not it will seem as if you have come across a dragon at the entrance to a sacred cave. Confronting a dragon, once you have the sword of understanding in your hand, becomes more like a game than a life-threatening pursuit and what we might find in the cave is a pearl beyond price.

This book is aimed at helping those who are confronting dragons, have been scorched by encounters with them, or want to know what might happen if they do. Understanding the nature of the test, the forces at work and the treasure that lies in the cave behind will give you the tools to deal with anyone with whom you have, or are likely to have, a difficult relationship. *These* people, believe it or not, are your soulmates. We will explode the *contemporary* interpretation of the myth of living happily ever after and turn what seems to be 'bad luck' in relationships into something positive and useful.

A soulmate is someone – *anyone* – with whom we have an intense connection. Someone who we can't ignore, no matter how hard we try. It may be that we can move away from having their physical presence in our lives, but still they tug some invisible string inside our being, insisting that even though we can't see them, they are still around. As long as these people remain in our lives, whether tangibly or intangibly, our emotional response to them and the thoughts, and possibly dreams, we have about them tell us there is unfinished business of the soul here. Their job, whether they know it or not, is to teach us something, and when we have understood the meaning and purpose of their presence in our lives, we can perhaps remove the thorn from our side. These soulmates are not lovey-dovey bedfellows. On the contrary, their task is not to encourage cosy complacency, but to put us through hoops of fire, to test and try us, sometimes to the point of driving us nearly insane. The maxim 'what we resist, persists' is irritatingly true – and is particularly relevant in the case of soulmate connections.

From the very beginning of recorded history intense connections between two people have not been an easy row to hoe, it seems. Starting with Adam and Eve, the whole of history is punctuated with soulmate liaisons that have been a far cry from walking off into the sunset together. There are the Egyptian Isis and Osiris, Antony and Cleopatra, Romeo and Juliet right through Héloïse and Abelard to the Duke and Duchess of Windsor, and the soulmate triangle of Prince Charles, Lady Diana and Camilla Parker-Bowles. No one could say that any of these characters slept on beds of roses as a permanent state of being. On the contrary, history was shaped because of the magnetic force that held one to the other in spite of external circumstances.

Vertical Learning Curves

My own personal interest in unravelling the business of soulmates has come from a blistering experience that contained agony and ecstasy in equal measure. I am not suggesting that my intense soulmate connection will change anyone's history except mine and his – and that it most certainly did. Here is the key to understanding these connections: they hold the potential for radical change, both spiritually and emotionally. There was a sense of intense connection to this other person and, at the same time, that something else was happening that was beyond us both. Our relationship made no logical sense, but then soulmate connections have very little to do with logic. I was fortunate at least in having the advantage of being able to apply (retrospectively) some of the knowledge I had acquired on my journey through life, most particularly the years I had spent at the Centre for Transpersonal Psychotherapy and working at the College of Psychic Studies in London. What I had learned enabled me to understand that there are no such things as chance encounters so, even if my experience wasn't exactly easy, my soul was telling me something. I also realised for myself the effect this relationship had on my body, as well as my soul. How intense emotion directly affects the chakra system, knocks it out of balance and creates physical problems. From my training as a shamanic practitioner I understand the interconnectedness of all things and that energy follows the thought that creates it. A shaman keeps his eyes open for 'signs' that appear to direct and guide his path. I ignored those signs, and there were plenty of them.

By the time I met this particular soulmate, I had come from living an isolated existence in the Kenyan bush to a flat in central London. I had done fifteen years of personal growth work and spiritual exploration. I was up to my neck (and no doubt beyond) in metaphysics. Chakras, auras, souls, past lives and ancient history were my everyday diet. I had long since given up reading fiction as I devoured everything I could lay my hands on that concerned psychology, psychism, magic, mystery and the nature of the universe. I had been on a crash course in consciousness expanding. I had seen tables rising, carnations manifesting from thin air, pencils writing without a visible hand holding them, forks bending, seeds germinating and people possessed. I worked among healers, psychics and spiritual teachers. I shared my flat with crystals, Tibetan bowls, runes and essential oils. I explored many avenues, and if I hadn't actually done it, then I'd probably got a book that could tell you about it. It was as if I were being given the tools to help me cope with what followed. These tools I will tell you about (in Chapter 7) so that if you find your-self in a similar situation, you won't have to go to your doctor to be told that you are having a breakdown and Prozac will sort it out.

Complementary practitioners of various kinds gave me the first aid that I needed, but the most important healing tool I had was my *understanding* of what had happened to me at every level of my being. I hope that the following pages will help you, too, to understand and find answers to the questions that we ask ourselves regarding intense connections to others. For me, as in the myth of Theseus and the Minotaur, there was always the sense that I had hold of a thread that would lead me out of the labyrinth I had had to enter in order to meet my deepest fears head-on. This thread was my sense of knowing that there was some kind of plan at work.

My soulmate epic was set against the backdrop of Egypt. It was a more intense and, ultimately, frightening experience than most people will ever have to confront, but it gave me the invaluable personal understanding that no matter how difficult or painful a relationship may be, there is a priceless gift wrapped up in the middle of it. The deeper the experience, the greater the opportunity for fundamental changes to be made and the more wrapping paper that is removed, the sooner the gift is revealed.

On my third visit to Egypt in five months – I had become fascinated by the country – I encountered the man who was to turn my life (including my bank balance) upside down. Our first meeting was not especially remarkable except for the fact that I made a mental note of what I considered to be an over-confident and somewhat arrogant attitude being expressed by this tall, handsome man. He was the assistant manager on a five-star Nile cruiser and responsible for the 'Welcome on Board' spiel given to all tourists on their arrival as they sip their hibiscus flower tea. I remember that he made a remark about the necklace I was wearing. No claps of thunder, flashes of lightning, not even a small peal of bells – yet.

We had a week on the boat and I was getting increasingly frustrated with the answers I was getting from the Egyptologist on board to my many questions, particularly his interpretation of the hieroglyphic symbols and the literal explanations of things that clearly had a metaphysical symbolism. I stood at the desk in the lobby of the boat after a trip to one of the temples. The tall, handsome 'Welcome on Board' man was on duty. 'Why won't somebody tell me the *truth* about Egypt?' I wailed.

'What truth?' he replied.

'Don't tell me this peculiarly shaped sceptre, the *uas*, that you see everywhere with its two prongs and weird animal's head on top is just a walking stick! What is it?'

'It's used for pulling the soul from the body after death,' he replied, as if he were telling me what time breakfast was. 'There are some secrets about Egypt that the people here don't understand.'

Oh! Someone was at last telling me something different. I had another look at this man. Dark – he is Nubian – with a finely sculpted face, balding on top, rather prominent forehead, beautifully shaped eyebrows, and lashes that would have done justice to an Aberdeen Angus. There was a wedding ring on his left hand. I imagined a lithe and beautiful wife attending to him when he was off duty. He told me later that he wore the ring to stop 'women getting the wrong idea' about him. That evening he joined me on deck for a mint tea, after my elderly uncle (with whom I was travelling) had retired to his cabin, and we were still sitting there at 2.30 a.m. The next day he said he hadn't been able to sleep as he'd never had a discussion like that in his life. Our evening debates continued for the few remaining days we had on board. I felt as if I were becoming magnetised by this man. Although he was extremely good-looking, it was not a sexual attraction that held me, but a tremendously strong sense that we had so much to say to each other that there would never be enough time to cover all the topics we had on our agenda. He would often say to me, later on, 'Sue, I have so many things I must tell you. I don't know if we have the time . . .'

In my previous relationships I had always longed for an intensity that I never seemed to find. I wanted to be at the top of someone's list of important things, but had always seemed to find myself down there among doing the accounts, mending the boat or tending sick cows. I had always longed for mad, passionate spontaneity and to be 'seen'. This is a core issue for me and had been kick-started in this lifetime by the death of my father in the Second World War when I was three months old. My mother fell apart – they adored each other – and I imbibed her grief, pain and fear through the very milk that kept me alive. Somehow I felt responsible for her pain, and didn't know how to make it better. We lived with my grandparents, and Grampa was an authoritarian figure who did not like noise and exuberance. 'Ssh! Here's Grampa home. Stop playing the piano now and go up to bed.' So this longing to be seen by a man came from the fact that I never was. I used to think there had been some terrible mistake, and that one day my father would walk through the door and everything would be all right. Unconsciously I looked for his face in every man I met.

Recognition, intensity, having meaning for someone was what I yearned for.

Three months after meeting this Egyptian soulmate I had formed a company, called Remember Egypt Ltd, of which he was a director, and before a year was out we were welcoming our own clients to Egypt to give them a different experience from the ones offered by tour operators. By this time we had fallen in love and got married in a London mosque, since it was illegal, according to Islamic law, for us to live together in Luxor without being married. As I said, it made no logical sense on any earthly level. Twenty-five years my junior, a devout Muslim from a poor but dignified background, he was a highly intelligent, charismatic, amusing, sensitive and observant companion. But, as I was later to find out, he was also volatile, possessive, obsessive and violent.

At thirty-two, he said that he needed intensity, commitment and total dedication – exactly what I searched for myself. Even in the darker days that followed, the world would disappear when we were together. It was all-consuming, this relationship. There was no spare energy for anything else. When we were not together he would play special songs to me over the phone, then fax me the words. He would send strings of cards that poured through the letterbox with one-liners of love written in his spider scrawl. He wanted more and more of everything, it seemed. At first this felt as if I were floating in a bath of honey. When we were together I could not take my eyes off him. The shape of that neck, the curve of the eyebrow – always straining to try and remember why all this was so familiar. It was the marriage of our minds that held me. He was always ready for a discussion about anything under the sun. We once spent seven hours non-stop, talking about life and its meaning. But I was a wounded bird, alighting on his open hand, and the sustenance that I had perceived I would find there became a poison, as the hand closed round me and I lost my ability to fly at all.

His attention to me started to move into obsession. Everyone from our clients and friends to the taxi driver and hotel waiters became a source of his jealous rages. In the end I felt like a mesmerised rabbit bewitched by a weaving snake. I had ignored the signs, which had begun not long after we met. The little flat I was living in burst into flames for absolutely no apparent reason one weekend when I was away. It then became infested with pharaoh ants which seemed to tramp out of every crack and socket. This infestation in the heart of London continued for three years – the same three years that I was involved with my Egyptian soulmate. I had bought a minuscule pied-à-terre in an attempt to generate some rental income, but, inexplicably, water suddenly appeared to seep through one of its walls and no one could find its origin. Then the Inland Revenue decided to investigate my income tax return and, to cap it all, on his first visit to England this man I seemed to be glued to nearly killed us both as a result of one of his uncontrollable rages. There were other things that I believe were all tied into the 'story'. My son who lives in Kenya had his house razed to the ground by a freak fire on my birthday three years to the month after I met this soulmate and at the actual time I had been born, losing his and his partner's entire personal history. I was then involved in a legal battle which resulted in a high court hearing. And so it continued, until the healing began five whole years after I'd first stepped on the soil of Egypt.

The cracks in our relationship began to appear fairly soon after we started living together in Luxor. As we all know, love is blind and although my friends and family clearly thought this, most of them said nothing. Not that I would, or could, have listened. I thought I had found a partner at last who lived life with a passionate intensity for the same things as I had. I was spending five or six months in Egypt with him and running our business, and then returning to my work in England in the summer when it got too hot to breathe in Luxor. He would then come over and spend a couple of months with me. It can't have been easy for him, trying to balance his ingrained beliefs about women and their place and position in society with how he perceived me and my very independent lifestyle.

The cracks widened into fissures until there was hardly twenty-four hours without explosions, interrogations and crockery-shattering eruptions. Fear became my constant companion. The tighter his grip on me – endorsed by his own insecurities – the less able I became at defending myself until, finally, after he had come just too close to actually ending my life, I asked one of my sons to come out to Egypt to help me get out of the tangle I was in. He is a mediator, this elder son of mine, and was very fond of my wild Egyptian partner, unlike my other son who had felt a strong and instant dislike the moment they met. We decided the best policy was to wait until my dark knight would be away on a desert trip with a client. I would tell him that I had to make an urgent ten-day trip back to England. I did this, but my ticket was one way. I left the beautiful domed farmhouse he had built for me from 90,000 mud bricks, said goodbye to my camel, water buffalo and donkey. I buried the gold ring he had given me with our initials etched in hieroglyphs under the mandarin tree outside our kitchen window and, although I felt half dead, I knew that I was lucky to be alive.

I had never believed in curses, thinking they belonged to medieval mindsets, but I have changed my belief about that, too. The fact that this was indeed a curse was endorsed by a remarkable complementary practitioner called Philip Tarr, who I consulted a year after I had left Egypt. He confirmed what I knew in my bones: namely that my relationship with this soulmate had started in antiquity. We had met in many previous lifetimes, but in ancient Egypt, around 2500 BC, he and a fellow priest/sorcerer had placed a curse on me involving power and politics. It had come 'alive' again in the here and now in order for us to release the limiting power it held us in – he as a perpetrator and I as a victim.

If it was indeed a curse that had come down through the ages, it was also a (heavily disguised) blessing. It dredged up my worst fears: of confrontation and standing my ground when challenged, threatened and abused by an extremely powerful person who I had started out by loving passionately. Our relationship had been a mix of pain and laughter in unequal quantities, which had drained me of everything. And this 'draining' was the most important part of it all. The tougher the nut, the bigger the hammer required to crack it open, revealing what is inside. In the three short years I had with this soulmate, I learned more about the hidden aspects of myself (that I would rather not look at) than I had done in the rest of my life put together. He did me the greatest favour anyone can do for any other: he made me look deeply at myself, evaluate my life and, as a therapist, see if I could really walk my talk.

For many years, through my work, I had had the opportunity to experience at first hand many people's encounters with soulmates of every possible variety. This enabled me to understand how difficult relationships always have the soul behind them, asking us to unmask our ego and personality to reveal our true selves. Getting stuck in blame, regret, bitterness, recrimination and guilt do nothing to free the soul from its unfinished business. In fact these emotions compound the situation. The more understanding you have of the dynamics that are at work, the easier it will become to understand painful, abusive, controlling and just plain difficult relationships. Or the sort of experi-ence I had myself, which felt as if I had suddenly entered the asteroid belt.

What This Book is All About

Through the following pages I hope you will find a map that helps to chart the turbulent waters of intense con-nection with whomever it may be. As I've said already, soulmates are not always bedfellows or of the opposite sex. They may be mothers-in-law, siblings, bosses, grannies, colleagues or parents – in fact anyone with whom we have an intense connection that is impossible to ignore. If we walk away from whatever it is a relationship is asking us to face, whether it is fear, loss of control, lack of com-passion, isolation or any one of the numbers of issues that the soul is asking us to address, then we are missing a truly valuable opportunity to learn about our selves and our true nature.

If this all has a ring of doom and gloom about it, take heart! Meeting a difficult soulmate will be the best thing that ever happened to you, once you understand the dynamic, and *everybody* will meet at least one in their lifetimes. These are the dragons that we attract towards us because they must be faced before we can enter the gateway to lives to be led more fully, with more awareness and, yes, more joyfully. With understanding, we can take off the armour of many lifetimes conditioned by pain, suffering and irrelevant belief systems so that we can fly, and soulmates are vital instructors and guides on our journey of becoming who we *really* are.

There is a vast ocean of people on the planet of every shape, colour and creed, and in order to begin to understand why we are drawn to, or have, specific individuals in our lives, we will begin at the beginning by having a look at what we mean by 'soul'. It's a word much used these days, but not really understood and if we don't really know what the soul is, how can we talk about it having a mate? Finding out what a soulmate is, exactly, and how such a relationship came into being in the first place will help get things into perspective and answer the sorts of questions you may have about them. Soulmates come in different guises and are sometimes confused with a 'twin flame' but they are not the same. I will explain the difference here. The *history* of our soul is always involved with soulmates, so we will then explore the matter of past lives and how the law of karma is involved in these encounters. Since our soulmate connections are invariably with those we have met or been with before, an understanding of the role that karma and past life dramas play in soulmate connections helps to bring illumination to the situation. I have included a chapter on the chakra system, which may find you wondering what on earth the chakras have to do with soulmates – and the answer is everything! Each chakra is 'encoded' with information about the state of our physical, emotional and spiritual well-being. Soulmates press our buttons – that's why they are in our lives – and understanding what's underneath our reaction is one way to stop it repeating.

Then you will find a chapter on how to identify your soulmates and, most importantly, how to cope with the situation. I have also used quite a lot of quotations from the works of people who have walked this path before us. They act as telegrams from a higher power and encapsulate the point being made.

It is my sincere hope that the information contained in the pages of this book will help you to understand what is going on 'behind the scenes' in difficult and painful relationships. It will help you to understand that these soulmates shout a wake-up call to your soul, and they are helping you to prepare for a reunion that will be beyond your wildest dreams.

> *Out beyond ideas of wrongdoing and rightdoing,*
> *There is a field. I'll meet you there.*
> *When the soul lies down in that grass,*
> *The world is too full to talk about.*
> *Ideas, language, even the phrase 'each other'*
> *Doesn't make sense.*
> JALALUDDIN RUMI

In my work over the past years, I have run many classes and workshops, and seen hundreds of people on an individual basis. I have learned from this experience that it's never possible (or appropriate) to predict what anyone's history may contain – only their own soul knows. In the past one hundred years we have moved from Freudian analysis to every form of therapy imaginable, most of which is not soul-centred. I have found that past life regression can be an extremely powerful and life-changing way for people to understand and bring perspective to their current problems, but this, too, seems to be changing. At the end of the day, past lives are simply one-act dramas of the soul.

Increasingly, the most important part of a regression is when the client relives the experience of the soul leaving the body it has just been occupying and returns to its place of origin, giving the client a real and valid experience of their spiritual nature that goes beyond the problems of life on our planet. Here, in this state of consciousness, it is possible to meet with others from your soul family, including your soulmates, in order to bring understanding, love and compassion to any situation. Accessing the inter-life state also has a profound effect on those who have a fear of death and dying. It's becoming easier for us to access our 'archives' and it is really encouraging to notice that those who are seeking more knowledge and information about themselves include a large proportion of young professional people from many different backgrounds.

The answers and secrets about life really are within each of us, if we can dare to explore the inner passageways of our selves.

what is the soul?

Defining the Undefinable

All day I think about it, then at night I say it.
Where did I come from, and what am I supposed to be doing?
I have no idea.
My soul is from elsewhere, I'm sure of that, and I intend to end
  up there.
Who looks out with my eyes? What is the soul?
I cannot stop asking.
If I could taste one sip
Of an answer, I could break out of this prison for drunks.
I didn't come here of my own accord, and I can't leave that way.
Whoever brought me here
Will have to take me home.

JALALUDDIN RUMI

Before embarking on the subject of soul*mates*, we need to understand more clearly what we mean by 'soul'. If you stopped people in the street and asked them what this word meant to them, you would probably get a range of responses from simply, 'I don't know,' to 'Something that links me to God.'

Trying to describe the soul is like putting a bird in a box. It's like trying to describe a dream, or something we can't quite grasp, something that is mysterious and just beyond our reach of comprehension. For a start it's difficult to comprehend the fact that the soul is eternal – it goes on for ever and ever – while our bodies and personalities are temporary vehicles and masks that are designed specifically so that the soul may *evolve* through experience on earth. I remember as a child asking, 'Where does the sky end?' and being told that it has no end. These are the sort of questions, like, 'What was before the beginning?' that pop the fuses in our little finite minds. It is as if we have factory-installed hardware that simply cannot understand an infinite reality.

One theory about the beginning of everything is that once upon a time we were just pure formless energy. At some point the One Mind, God, the Creator of all that is needed to know itself. In order to know something fully, it must be experienced and experienced consciously. Folded within the source of everything was a tremendous love and the *desire* to express this.

Existing in a state of stasis does not encourage anything to know itself. Everything is born from an idea. From a palace to a planet, there first has to be a blueprint, a plan, or how else can it come into being? The blueprint or design then gives something form in the physical, material world, but as we create it, we may decide to make certain alterations depending on the conditions that are experienced during the creation. Something like building a house when, once we begin to lay the bricks and mortar, we have to make alterations to the architect's plan which may not have taken into account the prevailing weather or local materials available. These conditions define the outcome, but cannot be known until whatever it is comes into being.

So the One divided itself, in order to know itself, express its love, and eventually our souls came into being. Our souls are fundamentally like cells, informing the greater body of which they are a vital part. I would not know that I had touched a hot plate unless the cells in my finger-tips informed me. In order to understand anything, experience of it is a fundamental requirement – we are the sensors for the Creator's experience.

The ancient hermetic maxim 'As above, so below' may help us here. In other words the macrocosm is reflected in the microcosm. Within our bodies are trillions of cells. Similarly, each one of us is a 'cell' within the body of humanity. Our planet is a cell within the solar system and the solar system a cell within our galaxy and so on, ad infinitum. Even the cells within our bodies, with their orbiting electrons and protons replicate our solar system in microcosm. As Plato observed:

> *perhaps there is a pattern set up in the heavens for*
> *one who desires to see it, and having seen it,*
> *to find one in himself.*

So all those aeons ago, the One gave birth to souls without number in order to experience itself. Down and down we came, from the pure energy of formlessness into differentiated beings of light. Each atom of the One contained the polarities of negative and positive in comple-mentary perfection, symbolised by the ancient symbol of yin and yang. Each half, though different, contained the essential seed of the other. Then, according to the ancient texts, another split occurred: the separation of the yin from the yang, and here we find the fundamental 'wound' of separation that each of us carries deep, deep within our soul being. This separation was a vital experience on the soul's journey, in order for each of us to become individuated beings. This is the source of our yearning for union, and our search for the love that we once knew, the feeling of being so close to another that it feels as if we are extensions of each other. We look for this reunion in the physical form of a soulmate.

Continuing their evolutionary journey, these separated 'cells' then formed into clusters, or soul groups, each group working on a particular *theme* and consisting of anything between fifteen and one hundred souls who elected to experience life on earth, for example. Other souls and groups will have chosen to have different experiences in different parts of the One's 'multiverse'. Since we are interested in our own experience and its meaning, what is happening in the multiverse is not information we have access to at the moment. Our souls are having an earthly experience in order to find out what it is like to be contained within a dense physical body, governed by the laws of gravity and duality. Our internal computers are fitted with limited equipment, which means that there are certain things, such as the concept of infinity, that we are not capable of understanding. We see things in a limited, finite way in a time-bound reality. In other words, when we are in our human bodies, it seems as if we are moving along a line in time which has a past, a present and tomorrow or the next second is the future.

In these physical bodies we are also governed by the laws of gravity and polarity. What does that mean? Gravity literally keeps our feet on the ground, and the law of polarity or duality ensures that our understanding of everything is *relative*. I know only that the weather is fine today because I compare it with the 'bad' weather of yesterday. We measure our life and its experience by relating it to something that we already know. It is not so in the spiritual realms where these laws do not apply. These polarities, or dualities, provide the basic themes that your soul and its group will be working on and I will explain this in more detail in the chapter on karma and reincarnation, but let's say for now that you are working on the theme of power. The opposite of this is power-lessness. You will have had many incarnations experiencing all aspects of power and the lack of it. In one life you will be an aggressor, in another a victim, until ultimately you realise neither of these polarities defines you and they then come into balance. Or you may be working with the poverty/abundance polarity. Experiencing both ends of this, lifetime after lifetime, culminates in the realisation that you, as a soul, can never be impoverished, nor does material wealth necessarily make you more aware of your spiritual nature.

Soul Themes

It may not feel like a gift, of course, but any event that carries a 'charge' is sure to give you a clue about the theme your soul and its mates are working with. This theme will appear consistently in past lifetimes, although sometimes we are given a couple of lifetimes' respite. Each and every soul belongs to a group, and the members of each group work with a particular theme, which will run through most incarnations. So if we take the theme of power as an example again, we will experience every configuration of being power*ful* and power*less*. Perhaps we have had a lifetime where we used our power for our own personal gain and we abused the power that we had. Then we need to experience what it is like to be overpowered by another. We may be working on the theme of health, and its absence, or wealth and struggling with poverty, or love. Here is a checklist of some of the major themes:

Abandonment	Guilt
Forgiveness	Justice
Betrayal	Trust
Persecution	Intimacy
Exile and belonging	Sexuality
Judgement	Power
Poverty	Freedom
Spirituality	Disease

Any of these issues may be brought into sharp focus in our relationship with others. These others, who may be key players in any of the themes, will be members of our soul family. They will be the soulmates with whom we have drawn up our pre-incarnation contracts in order to bring the theme into focus.

Soul Groups and Families

Our soul group or family is something like a wagon train within which it is required of each soul to experience all the different roles existing within the collective of the wagon train. The soul changes roles in each incarnation in order to experience life in all its myriad forms and its particular theme from every angle. Within this wagon train there will be those souls, or a particular soul, with whom you have a stronger connection. You have spent many lifetimes together in close relationships – rivals, parents, lovers, masters, slaves and siblings – working on your particular theme on earth. The information of your experience is then taken back to your soul family for evaluation and decision-making regarding how your next incarnation might expand your experience and understanding of the theme. Not all our soul family will be down here on the earth plane at the same time. Some of those in our soul group or family will be more closely connected to us than others, but all in our soul family are concerned with the conscious experience of being contained within a dense physical body and ultimately for body and soul to exist in total harmony. Harmony of body and soul, when we attain this perfect balance, will mean that we have mastered the nature of duality. In other words, balancing the opposites. Heaven and earth will coexist at last. We will understand the nature of right and wrong, black and white, you and me, and see that they are not separate polarities, but simply different aspects of each other.

When our hearts are as light as feathers, and the affairs of the earth no longer knock us for six, we will be ready for the next conscious experience elsewhere. In the meantime, there is unfinished business to be dealt with here and now, and soulmates are fundamental to clearing and cleaning accumulated residues from the past. But if life on earth is all about our soul collecting experience, how are we supposed to know what the soul is searching for?

Why Don't Our Souls Make Their Presence Felt?

One of the obstacles we face in understanding, and indeed knowing, more about our soul and its purpose is that our awareness has become extremely limited. We live, love and experience life in this human body in a very narrow band of sensory perception. Our visual range is limited to the spectrum of the colours of the rainbow, but we also know there is ultraviolet and infrared which exist either side of the rainbow range. How many more hues might there be? Our ears can only cope with sounds within an extremely limited auditory range. Too low, and we simply do not hear them; too high and our eardrums would explode in the way that a wine glass does when a soprano hits a certain high note. Our senses of smell and taste are similarly limited.

There is another reason why we have become unaware of the presence of our souls and that is because within our brain there are two hemispheres. It is as if we have twin travellers housed within our craniums, each with a very different function but both essential to our understanding and interpretation of physical and non-physical reality. To explain how they both work, we can use the example of doing a jigsaw, which requires input from both hemispheres. The right brain holds the vision of the picture on the lid of the box, and the left brain sorts out the pieces into colour and section. It's like life, really. Our right mind holds the vision of our life, and the left sorts out the details to make it happen. The relevance of this to our understanding of our soul nature is because the soul speaks to us through our 'right' minds. And if we cannot hear the voice of our soul, how are we ever to know that it exists?

Through the right brain, we can access our imagination, our dreams, our intuition and a consciousness that is out of time-bound reality. It is from here that we get our source of inspiration. The visionary Sufi poet, Jalaluddin Rumi, understood this when he said:

> *If you can't go somewhere,*
> *Move in the passageways of the self.*
> *They are like shafts of light, always changing*
> *And you change when you explore them*

When the two halves are used in tandem, there is balance. Being too rational makes life dry and dusty, but being too 'right-brained' will make us seem like a space cadet: airy-fairy and ungrounded.

While we predominantly rely on our left brain, we will believe that everything has a beginning, a middle and an end – it is finite and linear. Understanding the difference between the two sides of our brain and their different functions will help us to understand how our soul communicates with us, and what stands in the way of this communication. Our souls are only a thought away.

However we might try to define the soul with labels and structure, according to the dictates of the left brain, perhaps we all understand that it is the source of our deepest feelings. If we give ourselves 'heart and soul' to someone or something, we are giving to the utmost of our capabilities and there are certain qualities that differentiate these feelings from everyday emotions. When we feel something 'deep down inside' us, when we just 'know' something, then we are in touch with our soul.

Where Are You, My Soul?

Realising how narrow our understanding of our selves is – body, mind and soul – will help to expand the awareness of our soul's presence. The soul is 'attached' to the body by what is sometimes referred to as a silver cord. It has been perceived by psychics and sensitives and those who have had near-death experiences. When it is time for the soul to leave earth, this cord becomes detached from the body, freeing the soul to return home. But while it is busy with its experience on earth, the soul will form part of our energy field.

Everything that exists has an energy field, which varies according to what you are. A boulder will obviously have a different field surrounding it from a buffalo. The more animate and alive something is, the bigger and more variable is its energy field.

If we could see our own auric field, we would see our physical bodies surrounded by an oscillating 'cloak' of many colours which vary according to our own personal weather. Our auric field has several layers to it, which all interface with one another and have different rates of vibration. The physical part of us – our bodies – is obviously the densest, and exists at a low frequency of vibration. The next layer is known as the 'etheric double' which is measurable and which varies in strength according to our physical health. This layer can be photographed, using a method called Kirlian photography, named after the two people who discovered what became known as the 'phantom leaf effect'. Using specialised cameras, they took a photo of a healthy leaf and then, having chopped off a part of the leaf, photographed it again. The picture revealed the same outline as if the leaf were whole, thus proving that an energy matrix surrounds us. It was also discovered that ill health, or low energy, could be detected in this matrix that surrounds every living thing before disease actually manifested itself in the body.

Moving outwards, the next 'layer' or level of our subtle anatomy is the astral, or emotional body. Understanding this emotional layer of our auric field is crucial for life in general and soulmates in particular since this is where our feelings are registered. Our feelings drive our behaviour and are themselves driven by our egos and personalities rather than our soul. This is where we are aware of someone pressing our buttons, hitting our 'raw nerves' or 'touching our hearts'. Feelings can make us expansive, or shut us off from the world. What happens in our feeling department is largely based on our history, and I don't mean only in this lifetime. Most of our emotions are reactions – action re-plays – or knee-jerk responses to people and situations. We feel good if someone says something nice to us and hurt if we get the opposite. When it is time for the soul to leave this body, the astral or emotional layer shatters, leaving the soul to return home free of all the millions of emotions that were experienced in that lifetime. Deep emotional trauma, however, creates what is known as a *samskara*, or 'scar' on the soul: I will explain more fully in Chapter 3. These *samskaras* are often inextricably linked with our soulmate connections.

Moving out from the body then, and finer in vibration than the astral level, is the third field of energy that makes up the aura. This is the mental body, where our thoughts register. Our thoughts connect with the emotional body, and we then experience the results of this connection. For example, you might wake up one bright and beautiful day, jump out of bed feeling full of life, and your mind says, 'You were worried about something yesterday. What was it? Oh, yes, you have to fill in your income tax forms today.' Suddenly the sun clouds over and your energy field contracts. All that happened because of a thought.

Our thoughts, like our feelings, create a lot of static in the auric field on a daily basis, so no wonder we are not aware of the next level of our subtle anatomy, which is our spiritual, or soul 'body'. This has the finest vibration of all the levels discussed so far. Our physical body is sensory, our emotional body 'feels' things, our mental body registers our thoughts, but our soul just 'knows'. This most important level of our being is the one that gets the least attention. It is not pushy, does not make demands on our attention like the unruly children that are our thoughts and feelings. But even though we may not be aware of the presence of our soul, it has a quiet determination and all the patience in the world. It is continually looking for opportunities to make itself known and has electromagnetic qualities to assist it in its task.

Your soul is here for a reason and that reason must be addressed. The magnetic aspect will draw towards you the people and situations needed to be experienced, and the electrical part is responsible for your response. Again 'what we resist, will persist'. We continually magnetise situations towards us, but our reactions are repeatedly governed by the wayward children in the astral and mental bodies – our thoughts and feelings under direction from the ego. 'Here's another chance to respond from the heart,' says the soul. 'Oh no!' say the ego and personality in unison. 'How can we trust a high-flyer like you?' And so it goes on. If we don't get the message, and mostly we don't, then the soul will persevere, often increasing the stakes, until finally we open our eyes and lead our lives more soulfully. Having your soul in the driving seat of your life changes everything. Communication with your soul on a regular basis builds trust in its wisdom and guidance. Giving a little time (and it doesn't have to be hours of meditation) and space to let the frantic static of thoughts and feelings calm down allows the airwaves to clear so that we can hear that 'still, small voice' that has so much to say if we can only get ourselves out of the way.

Why Have We Forgotten?

If I am a soul having a human experience, why have I forgotten who I really am? Why can't I remember where I came from and why isn't my soul a more effective pilot? Forgetting was part of the plan, because we would not have known what it was like to be fully human if we were still totally in touch with our spiritual nature.

One of the factors responsible for our spiritual amnesia is that everything in our known universe is cyclical. We are aware of the clock that ticks through seconds, minutes, hours, seasons, tides and lifetimes. These are all tiny clocks that tick within much greater cycles of which we are unaware. These great cosmic clocks relate to the evolution of our collective spiritual consciousness. For the last fifty years people have been 'waking up' to their spiritual selves. Or rather the spiritual, soulful side of us has heard the alarm and is preparing to get out of bed to live a very different day. At this moment in time, it seems that the hands of various cosmic clocks are approaching 'midnight' at the same time.

One of the clocks that is particularly interesting is the Cycle of the Yugas – the Hindu idea of world cycles. These have their equivalent in the classical Greek and Roman myth of the four ages. We are currently at the end of the last of these four ages, or quadrants on the clock face, which is known as the Age of Kali, or the Kali Yuga. Kali is the Hindu goddess of time and destruction and her epoch takes us down into the underworld where we become spiritually comatose. It is the time on this great cycle when we are the furthest away from our spiritual nature, having become more involved with and attached to our existence in physical form. It is symbolised by iron, warfare, density, materialism and suppression of the feminine. As it draws to a close, history appears to repeat itself. But it is coming to an end, concurrent with the dawning of the Age of Aquarius – which also heralds the beginning of another cosmic cycle.

As we get closer to the point where everything will change and are being presented with an opportunity to move to the next level, we can feel the effects. It is happening in front of our eyes at this moment: religions pitched against one another and medieval reruns of pestilence, droughts and floods. Even the earth itself seems to shake. It is as if we are being forced to look at and remember the stages that lead up to the end, and collectively regurgitate our past in order to free our spirits. We have become 'bogged down' in our karmic backlog.

You may be wondering what all this has to do with the soul, but the point is that as we have moved round this great cycle, we have had hundreds of different incarnations, and become progressively entranced with our experiences on earth rather than remembering that we are fundamentally *spiritual* and not physical beings. Our soul-mate encounters play a key role in helping us rub the sleep from our eyes.

It would also seem as if the very ground beneath our feet, the earth itself, is deeply involved in this transformative process. It is sounding its own alarm to wake us up. Nicola Tesla, a brilliant and visionary scientist, discovered in his research at the turn of the century that the earth essentially functions as a massive planetary capacitor, storing and releasing electrical charge at specific intervals. This planetary 'pulse' became known as the Schumann Cavity Resonance, after the German scientist who continued Tesla's work in the 1950s. It is believed that this heartbeat of the earth was stable for several thousand years at 7.8 Hz or cycles per second. Interestingly, this is approximately the same pulse as the brain emits when in an alpha or semi-conscious state, such as when we drift off to sleep or in a semi-trance. Has the earth been dozing? By 1998 this pulse had increased to 9.5 Hz and is still increasing.

Not only is the ground beneath our feet changing its frequency, but the magnetic field around the planet is *decreasing*. It has happened approximately fourteen times before in the last $4\frac{1}{2}$ million years when the magnetics have dropped to zero. This decrease means that the 'glue' of human consciousness is destabilised and although it may feel uncomfortable, it offers an opportunity to release the old paradigms concerning home, family, career and life purpose.

What all these factors are effecting is a 'wake-up' call. Quite literally we are being shaken into rethinking who and what we really are. Some of the effects of the earth changes, as the giant clocks tick towards midnight, are being experienced by humanity as:

> The nature of time itself seems to have changed. Somehow there seems to be 'less' time. One could argue that the techno revolution plays a part in this but nevertheless it seems as if everything has accelerated.
>
> Our bodies are producing strange aches, pains, rashes and other anomalies. Legs, knees, necks and shoulders are particularly affected.
>
> Sleep patterns have become disturbed; we wake at odd times, particularly around 3 and 4 a.m.
>
> Our memories can't hold information in the way that they used to, and this has nothing do with age.
>
> There is a need for solitude, time to be by ourselves, and to put some distance between ourselves and our friends, family, groups or colleagues.
>
> Our dreams seem to have intensified.
>
> A loss of passion is being experienced.
>
> We often feel ungrounded and 'floaty'.
>
> There is a deep longing for many of us to return home.

All these symptoms indicate that change is in the air. It means the old has to be dissolved, or at the very least re-evaluated, whether we like it or not.

As our soul groups moved around the great cycle of evolving consciousness, we became more and more identified with the roles we played on earth rather than with our identities as an aspect of the One. We began to forget who and what we really are as we collected more unfinished business each lifetime until we became bogged down in our own karmic residues. Like a rainwater butt, which accumulates more and more dead leaves and bits and pieces every time it rains, there is now scarcely room for the water, or the presence of soul. But the ending of the Age of Kali encourages us to release, rather than accumulate more. What goes around seems to come around at an amazing rate, and our rainwater butts have been stirred deep down. We do not have to take everything that is solid out of this container – there is no time for that and it is not necessary, anyway. But what is required is that we identify ourselves with the nature of the water, rather than the accumulated detritus. This represents the essence of our soul, which has the ability to dissolve past residues through its eternal qualities of love and compassion.

Now we have come full circle from heaven to earth, from being wholly spiritual with no knowledge of how life would be contained in a human body, to being totally human with no real connection to our spiritual selves. It's time now for these two sides of us – body and soul – to work together as the team they were intended to be for our earthly journey. When we were pure light, we had no concept of how it would be to be contained in a dense, earthly vehicle, governed by the laws of gravity and polarity. We have travelled as far away from unity consciousness as we are ever likely to, and now we make our return, but carrying with us the *experience* of separation. We have completed a cycle on the spiral of evolving and have the opportunity of moving to the next level on the spiral, which is to become soul or self-realised individuals. Or we can repeat the process again, until we arrive at this point.

It's Time to Remember . . .

If we could remember what we have done and how we lived previous incarnations, this lifetime would be a totally different experience. But as our souls entered our bodies it was as if we went through a ring-pass-not. Access to our personal archives was not an option, and each life was started with a clean slate. Or was it?

Spiritual amnesia seems to have been part of the contract – until recently that is. Today's children are different. We have in our midst a whole new breed of individuals, some of whom have been called 'the Indigo Children', so named because their auric fields were observed by those who can see these things as being a different colour – indigo – from the rest of us. Their different auric fields reflect other differences which do not always make life easy for them. It's as if they cannot – will not – accept some of the rules and restrictions laid on them by current society. They seem unable to tell lies, computer technology is second nature to them, and many are diagnosed with Attention Deficit Disorder, or autism. It's almost as if they feel they have been born on the wrong planet. In fact there has been no mistake, they are here to help change things quickly and radically.

A woman told me not long ago of how her little three-year-old daughter said one day, 'I'm glad I chose you, Mummy, and not the other lady.'

Another mother recounted how her son Tommy refused to accept her as his mother. 'My mummy doesn't look like you, she looks different.'

'But Tommy, you came out of my tummy in the hospital.'

'No, I didn't. I came down on a light,' he said wistfully.

An American psychologist, Dr Stevenson, has collected a huge body of evidence in the case for reincarnation from interviews with over 2,000 children. He prefaced his enquiries with, 'How was it when you were big?' and received some astonishing replies. Detailed information about other families, in different places, even to the point, in some instances, of having an ability to speak a language they had never heard or come in contact with in this lifetime. His meticulous research has gone a long way to reinstate the belief in reincarnation as a fact rather than a fantasy.

If a new wave of children are coming into the world aware of who they really are, who will wake us, the older generations? The others from our soul family with whom we have strong links. We are not likely to pay attention to someone who doesn't affect us, because it's a wake-up call that we need. This may take the form of an alarm bell rung in our ears that we can't sleep through. The bell ringer will be a soulmate who might present themselves in unexpected guises.

what exactly is a soulmate?

Facts and Fantasies

The face of all the world is changed, I think
Since first I heard the footsteps of thy soul.
ELIZABETH BARRETT BROWNING

What does this word soulmate mean to *you*? When most people are asked this question, they are silent for a moment, and their voice seems lower and quieter when they answer.

'Someone who knows what you are thinking, without speaking.'

'Someone who you feel as if you have known for ever' (which you have).

'There are no barriers between soulmates.'

'Someone who accepts you, warts and all.'

Universally, it conjures up thoughts of a relationship that has a sense of timelessness about it – a 'knowing' of another that transcends the humdrum of everyday life; someone who transports us to a place of safety and containment where we are not alone.

Implicit in our perception of soulmate relationships is a sense of deep mutual understanding. This person, as Eva

37

Cassidy sings so beautifully, 'knows you by heart'. It is the feeling of being linked to another by a bond that defies earthly explanation. Someone who has always been with us, will never leave us and is our complement in every way. Our 'other half'? Does this mean that life without a soulmate is only half lived, and we must await an encounter with such a person through the arches of the years before we are truly alive? Why do we imagine such a person exists anyway? Our understanding of the word soulmate needs to be redefined.

Twin Soul or Soulmate?

The vast majority of us will not find that one-and-only person with whom we will live happily ever after, because that state cannot be permanent on earth. We will not get on with the job in hand – experiencing life in our human containers – if we sit gazing into another's eyes all day long. Happily ever after comes later, when we have been polished and rubbed (probably not in the way we would prefer) into shining brilliance by our earthly experiences, and our soulmates are the ones who will help us achieve this. The myth of the one and only, and the ensuing state of happily ever after, has its roots in our soul's history and there is confusion in people's minds between a soulmate and what is termed a *twin soul* or *twin flame*. This confusion leads to the expectation that a soulmate will fulfil us in the way that only a twin soul is able to. As the name implies, our twin flame is literally our twin. The yearning to be united with another comes from the memory of that time when we did exist in union and perfect harmony with our twin soul.

What exactly is a soulmate?

We have already looked, broadly, at the soul's history in Chapter 1. Let's take a deeper look to see how twin souls fit in. I will return to the ancient Chinese symbol for yin and yang to help explain the unexplainable. This symbol gives us an image to help the mind grasp a concept that is truly beyond our comprehension. First there is the circle, itself another universal ancient symbol meaning absolute unity and perfection. In the Chinese Tao this circle then divided itself with a serpentine line producing two comma-like shapes (here are our twin souls or flames) representing the division into opposite principles on which all things, beings, events and time periods are ordered. The yin principle corresponds to the negative, receptive, feminine, darkness, earth, passive, moon and wetness and the broken line seen in the hexagrams of the ancient oracle, the *I Ching*. The yang principle, on the contrary, corresponds to the positive, active, masculine, brightness, the sky, penetration and dryness and the unbroken line.

The separation of these two halves marked the beginning of duality and is represented in biblical mythology by Adam and Eve eating of the fruit of the Tree of Knowledge of Good and Evil (duality) and, as a result, being kicked out of the Garden of Eden. Women throughout the centuries have carried the burden of guilt for enticing Adam, with the help of the serpent (sexuality), into this demise. Did he not have a mind of his own? This was the beginning of dividing things into their polar opposites and our experience of duality. But although it would seem that everything has been divided into two separate compartments, within the middle of the darkness of the yin is a spot of light, and within the whiteness of the yang there is a spot of dark, representing the mutual dependency of both principles. Yin and yang are never fundamentally opposed to one another; rather, they constantly influence one another, each containing the seed of the other.

Imagine that these two halves of the circle have now separated, producing two tadpole-like individual energies which are fundamentally opposite, but also representing perfect balance and unity, and which now go forth into being to experience existence. First, simply to experience and then to become *conscious* of that experience. Held deep within each half of this original circle is the remembrance of that balance and unity from where the journey first began. It is because of the *memory* that each of us contains deep within us that once upon a time we existed in complete and total harmony with our complementary 'other', the yin of our yang or vice versa, that we hold on to the hope of returning to that sense of being totally connected once again. The image of that other becomes hazy after all this time of separation, but nevertheless it is *there*. And it is this hope of reunion with our twin soul or other half that we carry within us when we come to earth and try to find it in what we currently understand as 'our soulmate'.

But in this case, two halves will not make us whole. We must become whole in our own right, balanced *within* ourselves rather than without. It is an *inner* marriage – our inner soulmate – that our souls are seeking to find on earth which will lead to our wholeness (or holiness). And when these two individuated souls are finally reunited with each other – an inevitable event – there will be a union that defies description. But it rarely if ever happens on earth. Jesus, in his parable of the prodigal son, gives us a sense of the soul's journey from leaving the security of home (the heavens), losing its way and then ultimately returning as a very different being from the one who set out to find its fortune. Here is the story.

The Prodigal Soul

There was a rich man who had two sons, the younger of whom asks his father for his share of his father's estate. Within a few days of receiving this he has left home and cashed in his asset for money. He then proceeds to squander his inheritance on 'reckless living'. Before long he is penniless, and reduced to looking after pigs in order to survive. He realises that his father's servants have a better life than he, so decides to return home and confess to his father that he is not worthy to be called his son and perhaps his father could treat him as a paid servant. He sets out to return home, and is spied by his father who sees him approaching from a long way off, and his heart goes out to him. When his son arrives, he flings his arms around him and orders his servants to kill the fatted calf, and to bring the young man a fine robe and ring. 'For this son of mine was dead and has come back to life. He was lost and is found.'

Not surprisingly, the elder brother doesn't think much of this. After all, he's stayed at home, worked hard and never disobeyed his father and never even received so much as a fatted kid to share with his friends. Does this mean it's wrong to be responsible? No, the message here is that the younger son goes out into the world and is stripped of his material possessions (equivalent to the loss of his ego-self) which gave him his identity. Reduced to nothing, he finds humility and his reunion with his father is a deeper, more joyful and poignant experience because of this. This younger son – representing the soul – had become more of a man and a person because of that separation.

Our twin soul – our other half as it were – is the only one with whom we feel this sense of totality and unity. We search for it in the faces of others. Our longing for this reunion follows us through all our incarnations, through all our husbands, wives, lovers and mistresses. We fall in love – and then mostly fall out of it when it fails to fulfil the initial promise and expectation. Falling in love is like watching the trailer of a film. But somehow either we never actually see the film or it fails to live up to the promise of the trailer. Or it may be the agony of unrequited love, when one person's heart responds to the sound of another, but it seems the feelings are not reciprocated. This is not the stuff of twin souls.

Why is it that so little seems to be known about this? Because, like the prodigal son, we had to go off into our own individual wildernesses, not holding the thought of reunion, but of making it on our own. We must become 'whole' away from the security and safety of our soul family. It is the journey itself that is so important. Perhaps we would have led our many lives in a different way if we had known of this inevitable reunion. The purpose of relationship is to encounter and experience the nature of our personal limitations.

So we come to earth, always carrying the yearning for the other, longing for that reunion that will take away this pain of separation and, yes, loneliness. Now the Age of Kali and the energies of the dawning of the Age of Aquarius are weaving themselves into our collective souls. We have gone about as far as we can go into the density of matter and the amnesia of our soulfulness. There is a tremendous need for a return to that sense of unity that we have lost. This becomes evident in the collective outpourings that have been a hallmark of the past decade. We feel united in our grief about the outrages that take place around the world. The death of Princess Diana produced an unprecedented expression and outpouring of emotion; the murder and abduction of innocents has held people in its horrific thrall; and of course the event on September 11th shook the entire world, which people said 'would never be the same again'. Not to mention the enormous numbers of people who have got out of their armchairs to protest against war.

Does it have to be events of this magnitude to wake us from our sleep? National celebration or despair over the outcome of the World Cup and marches for the country-side all seem to draw people together, responding to a deep craving for this sense of unity, this sense of belonging to something. We have mistakenly felt that our sense of belonging would come from more and more belongings, but as our contemporary icons and idols fall from grace, it seems that belongings don't fill that hole in our being after all. So if this longing to be with our 'other half' belongs to our twin soul, and happily ever after is that state of union we will find only in the spiritual realms, what, then, is a soulmate?

A Soulmate is . . .

Another from your soul family with whom you have an intense connection. You will have had many incarnations together and a stronger bond than with others in your soul family. This connection may be wonderful, or extremely difficult. The difficult ones have the effect of a spiritual pan scourer and the wonderful ones are like being polished with a soft and beautiful duster. Both are equally important. It takes a Brillo Pad to loosen the residues of past cookery mishaps, overheating or too long on the stove, so that there is an encrustation that dims the lustre of the pot. Encounters with Brillo Pads can make you feel vulnerable, exposed, defiant, resistant, victimised, powerless, bitter, guilty, ashamed, disloyal, betrayed, humiliated or worthless, but it is *through* these windows of 'negative' feelings and emotions that we are offered the opportunity to see a view that contains their opposites. We draw our contracts up with these soul family members and others in our community before we take on another incarnation. Our parents, siblings, children and close friends on earth will certainly include a soulmate or two as well as, of course, our partners whether they are good, bad or indifferent.

'I would *not* have chosen these parents! Why would I choose a father/mother who abused me?' This is a tough one to come to terms with and for which there is not one single answer. As a victim of abuse, it may not be possible, in this lifetime at least, to forgive or even forget what happened, but the soul is asking the personality to take this experience to another level: that of understanding that nothing is accidental or coincidental, and nor does any action only involve one soul who is right and another who is wrong.

It is most likely that the abuser was abused themselves. It may be that this abuse, while horrific to experience and come to terms with in this lifetime, offers the soul an opportunity for a huge leap in understanding, an opportunity to exercise forgiveness towards someone who is obviously deeply involved with your soul group theme themselves. Perhaps, as a result, the abused person turns their traumatic experience into positive action such as helping others in a similar situation. It is also likely that the abused in this lifetime has been the abuser in a previous one, since we continually work with both ends of a theme.

We do not like to think that we could have been murderers, thieves or villains, but the chances are we have also played 'the bad guy' in some of our many soul dramas. The first time I personally accessed a past life experience of this sort, as a man who cut out the hearts of his victims, I refused to accept it. But the experience was vivid, and I could not deny it.

The whole business of soulmates is about growth and learning, and moving to a higher level of conscious awareness beyond the agendas of our egos and personalities. Knowing that I am this, but I can also be that and in the end I am neither. The strongest soulmates give us the hardest pushes, forcing us to go beyond our known boundaries of safety and fear. Not easy, but then a marathon runner does not do his training by sitting in a chair and watching TV. We cannot walk away from soulmates or ignore the situations that are created by their presence in our lives. If we do, the lesson we are refusing to look at will be presented in another form.

Our soulmates will feature in our lives wearing a variety of different hats and masks. Like a workforce of cleaners, there will be heavy-duty operatives and peripheral others. Your soulmates will be meeting with you in this lifetime

because you have drawn up a contract with them in the
spiritual realms and you meet each other because there are
lessons to be learned. This can be because:

> They are implemental in getting you to focus on an aspect of
> your soul group's theme.
> There is unfinished business between you.
> You owe them a debt or vice versa.
> Vows, promises and curses are involved which need releasing
> or completing.
> A desire to end tit-for-tat karma.

You will be drawn together by a 'tuning fork' effect
explained in more detail in Chapter 6. In other words there
will be a mutual resonance between you which may be
extremely uncomfortable, or it may be the 'love at first sight'
feeling. This provides the connection which keeps us in a
situation with them. Your soul knows what needs to be
addressed, so you will find yourself being drawn to places,
people and situations where the lessons and experiences will
then present themselves. Our relationships are the arena for
soul work. If you were a monk, sitting in a cave on a
mountain-top in self-imposed solitude, you would not learn
much about being a soul in a physical body and interacting
with others. It is through these interactions that we learn
about our own nature. The monk will not discover if he is
selfish, has control issues, can cope with intimacy, feels safe
in the world, or whether his heart dares to love another.

> *Only in relationship can you know yourself,*
> *not in abstraction, and certainly not in isolation.*
> J. KRISHNAMURTI

46

Soulmate Themes

There are some soul themes where soulmates play a more pivotal part than others. The themes of exile, poverty, disease or material loss may not have a key player but the following themes will certainly involve a soulmate.

Parent/Child	Sexuality
Forgiveness/Revenge	Freedom/Commitment
Betrayal	Love Triangles
Abandonment	Love/Hate
Power	

Parent/Child

This soulmate theme produces perennial princesses, those who need 'mothering', those who can't cut the apron strings, those looking for father figures in their relationships and those who treat another as if they were still a child. If this is your theme, your soulmate may or may not be your biological parent but, if so, will probably be the one of the opposite sex to you. Parents/soulmates of the same gender will be involved with you in a different theme (if there is friction) which might involve power or abandonment. Of course it's nice to go home and be Daddy's little girl, or have your mum looking after you, and there's nothing wrong in that as long as you are a grown-up in your other relationships with the opposite sex.

Forgiveness/Revenge

This really speaks for itself but this theme will involve either someone who has done something awful to you, or a situation where you have committed some 'crime' against another and cannot forgive *yourself*. Your soulmate here will be the one who wounds or the one you have wounded, and the challenge is to rise above the feelings of being hurt or wanting to get your own back, or the guilt for what you have done. Lives can wither from these feelings, which may have other aspects linked in such as betrayal, judgement and abandonment. It's no good pretending that the event that caused these feelings hasn't happened, but your heart (and soul) are asking you to let go of the pain, forgive and move on. Revenge simply keeps tit-for-tat karma perpetuating, until finally someone sees the futility in getting their own back. The soul is not interested in revenge – it is the business of the ego, who feels its authority has taken such a knock that there is only one way to redress the balance.

Betrayal

This is a common soulmate theme. Your partner goes off with someone else, you have your trust abused at work, you are sold down the river or lied to. This soulmate is not asking you to sit down and take whatever is thrown at you, but to assess the situation from your soul's perspective and not to shut down your ability to trust. It is important (and will be difficult) to confront them with what they have done without getting over-emotional. Speaking to them from the heart gives their soul an opportunity to realise the consequences of their action. If your partner has sexually betrayed you, it may be time to recognise that your relationship had run its course and neither of you were growing. Sitting down and being totally honest with yourself will stop you from attracting serial betrayers. Perhaps you can remember the story that hit the headlines some years ago about the wife of a prominent public figure who discovered that he was having an affair with a colleague? To help her cope with her hurt and fury at his betrayal, she cut up all his trousers and delivered his cherished collection of wine to all the neighbours in the village! No doubt in a previous lifetime she had responded to his betrayal in a much more damaging way or had been the betrayer herself.

Abandonment

Another difficult and painful soulmate theme which those who have had their babies adopted and those who are adopted themselves will be working with. The following story exemplifies the polarities of the abandonment theme being experienced in two consecutive lifetimes. Lydia is a dynamic thirty-eight-year-old woman who came for a past life regression to try and get to the bottom of her feelings that she had never really 'belonged' to anyone or anything. Since this issue must be addressed in this incarnation, she had chosen to be abandoned by her biological parents (soulmates) who were apparently untraceable. The theme kicks in. Although adopted at six weeks old by loving foster parents, her surrogate siblings (other soulmates from her soul family) reinforce her sense of not really being part of the family by saying things like, 'She's not *your* mummy, anyway, she's ours.' Because she *believes* that no one wants her, these deep feelings recreate this experience in her adult years by a series of relationships with men who leave.

This is what happened in her session with me. She begins the experience of the relevant past life as someone looking through a window from the outside. It is night time, and the scene she is observing is of a man and two small children who are clinging to each other. There is a Christmas tree which has been decorated and a fire burning in the hearth, but an overwhelming sense of sadness pervades the scene. She realises that she has no physical body – she is a ghost – observing the scene. She has been 'dead' for several days and tells me that she is the mother of the children and the beloved wife of the man. I ask her to go back in time, and the memories of life as part of this loving family come flooding back to her. The picnics, the family meals and the love of her husband, leading up to her sudden illness and ultimate death.

She moves through these events and then into the inter-life state, where she is reunited with the souls of her 'family' in the spirit world. And what a reunion that is. She also discovers that the three beloved members of her family in this past lifetime are her mother and adopted siblings in this one. They felt they had been 'abandoned' by her, through her death, in that lifetime. When the session is over, Lydia realises that her abandonment by her biological mother (a soulmate) is part of their contract: one to be abandoned and the other to abandon. Her adopted siblings, appearing to be cruel and exclusive, were two other soulmates, who had agreed to reinforce this feeling in Lydia, literally being cruel to be kind, and creating such pressure that she is driven ultimately to discover what the roots of this are and thus free herself into liberation from them.

Power

This theme will include soulmates who are control freaks, authority figures, victims, sadists, masochists and any soul drama where the master, slave, martyr and self-flagellating 'I am unworthy, I deserve to be punished' syndrome is found. Your soulmate involved with this theme will be helping you (and themselves) to work on the fact that power is not to be used to control others or give away, but to make a positive difference, however small, in the world. Beating yourself up is also a self-indulgent script that leaves you powerless. Bullies need victims and a victim mentality will draw a bullying soulmate towards it in order to create an opportunity to find its own power and authority. Saying, 'Thank you, but NO thank you,' means the victim has recovered.

Sexuality

Most people's ideas about soulmates include the union of bodies as well as souls, but soulmates are clearly not limited to those of the opposite sex or lovers of the same gender. However, it is in the arena of sexuality that hard-core soulwork will present itself. The longing for union that is carried within every soul can be filtered through the lens of sexuality which is, after all, the most powerful force within us and the only one that takes us 'out' of ourselves at the climax of orgasm. Our souls were called into existence through sexual union and all of us, without exception, have some knowledge of the subject. Our sexuality is not just a biological imperative to guarantee the survival of humanity, but also to experience the oneness that we have forgotten.

Sexual union with another is a sacred act, a million miles away from our current preoccupation with scandals, innuendoes, rapes, paedophilia, pornography, aberrations, incest and weird fantasies. Soulmates may be drawn to one another through a strong physical, sexual attraction in order for this chemistry to bind them together to address the real theme that will present itself later in the relationship. If, however, you are working on the theme of sexuality itself, it may manifest itself in an addiction to or repulsion of sexuality: it will be a preoccupation in your life. There is nothing wrong in choosing to live a celibate life, but the real reasons for this decision need to be on the table. The possibility for soul union is held within each sexual encounter, but it does not depend on positions, breathing techniques or particular practices according to a handbook, it is to do with love. Casual sex has the same nutritional value to the soul as fast food has to the body.

It is certain that the one you have been or are involved with is a soulmate, but whether this partner fulfils the sense of yearning in your soul after the magic has faded is another matter. Something drew you together, and that 'something' had good reason. Perhaps the attraction had to do with chemistry. It just felt as if your bodies belonged to one another – and the sexual union that ensued confirmed that this was 'meant'. Then the power of passion could not hold out against the power of the personality. Not enough glue in other areas to hold it together, and it fizzled like a rocket when it hit the ground, leaving you wondering how you could have felt the way you did. What happened to love in all of this? There is no act that is 'wrong' between consenting adults unless there is no shared love.

Freedom/Commitment

This theme may be brought to your attention by a soulmate who is restricting your emotional, financial or spiritual freedom. Or it may involve your ability to demand or reject commitment. Being contained by a soulmate can feel as if your wings are being clipped, if this is the theme of your soul. It is important to recognise the value in commitment, and not become a relationship butterfly, flitting from one to the next and always moving on when things start to get too intense. Perhaps you cannot allow your soulmate *their* freedom, and you need constant reassurance of their love and commitment to you. The lesson here is either to live together, allowing each other freedom for individual expression within the relationship, or to let them go to be themselves with another. The soul is asking you why you need another to make you feel safe. We need to remember that we are all evolving towards being individuated, unique souls in our own right.

Love Triangles

This is another and often extremely difficult soulmate theme, which involves three soulmates coming together to find a resolution that goes beyond 'possession' of another. If this situation has arisen in your life, then the three of you will have been playing musical partners through the ages. The connection between you all will be intense. If this time you are the one who is leaving a committed relationship, then you have to deal with what this makes you feel, but it is also vital to remember you are giving the one you leave the opportunity to move out of blame, revenge, anger and rejection. Nothing takes away the hurt, of course – we're human after all – but it is a major opportunity for growth.

Men and women often face huge moral crises when confronted with the choice between one soulmate who has lit their fire and another with whom there has been a committed relationship and possibly children. Prince Charles and the two women in his life is the most obvious contemporary example of a triangular soulmate situation, but these uncomfortable soulmate configurations have been recognised through the centuries. When the motivation to look for another is based on self-indulgence, boredom or escape from commitment, it does not evoke the soul searching that the story of King Arthur, Lancelot and Guinevere has mythologised. This tragic triangle is rooted in profound love on all sides, and teaches us that we can love people deeply in different ways.

Love/Hate

All soulmate encounters are asking us to move towards soul love in any situation. This is the story of Ian, someone who came for a past life regression in order to try and discover what the hateful relationship he had with his brother was all about. From the moment he was born his brother had hated him. He could even remember this brother leaning over his cot and pinching him as a baby. This continued through childhood, school and adolescence and grew into a powerful mutual animosity. Now in his late thirties, Ian – a psychotherapist – had not been able to get to the bottom of this relationship with his brother.

His past life recall (which is often like an internal video) opened on a battlefield. It seemed that everything was coloured with a red haze. Then he saw a figure to the left of him cut down by an enemy's sword. It was his younger brother. This young man in that lifetime was his elder brother in this. In that past life, Ian was a Nordic warrior, brave and fearless, who loved his younger brother with a deep and protective love. This was the first battle that he had taken him into, since he was barely a man, and as soon as he saw him killed, it was as if something snapped inside him. He went on a frenzy of killing, fuelled by his rage and grief and slaughtered literally hundreds of people without any sense of remorse. Finally he fell on his own sword, left his body and returned to his soul family where he was reunited with his 'younger' brother. What a reunion that was.

As a result of that past life where his love had resulted in such destruction, they had drawn up a pact that when they reincarnated again into different bodies that love must not be, since it led to such dire consequences. Now he realised that he and his brother are soulmates, experiencing both love and its opposite. He could have held on to the feeling of being persecuted by his brother, becoming a victim of another's 'bad' behaviour, until his dying day. Understanding that these 'negative' emotions actually have a positive intent changes the situation.

* * *

Soulmates

So, in summary, a soulmate is absolutely anyone with whom you have an intense connection. That connection is created by the magnetic quality of your soul, which draws you towards this person in order for you to take a long hard look – not at them, but at yourself. These mates have been around for ages and will continue to poke you in the ribs until you have woken up. They will continue to rub you up the wrong way until your heart is polished and the light of love shines out of you.

There have already been several references to our links with soulmates in previous incarnations, so we will now take a good look at how karma and reincarnation are involved in our soulmate liaisons.

past lives and karmic links

Haven't I Seen You Somewhere Before?

The soul passes from form to form, and the mansions of her
*   pilgrimage are manifold.*
Thou puttest off thy bodies as raiment, and as vesture thou dost
*   fold them up.*
Thou art from old, O soul of man,
Yea, thou art from Everlasting.
HERMES TRISMEGISTUS, *Egyptian Hermetic Fragments*

On its evolutionary journey, the soul has been here on earth many times before. It has decided which parents, culture, physical form and personality traits it will take on so that it can meet the challenges it needs in order to evolve. It has drawn up agreements with others from its soul group to create situations and to bring up emotions that need to be released, healed or expressed.

Understanding and exploring our past lives will give us further insights into our relationships with soulmates because they reveal the history behind these connections and give us a clearer idea of what our soul theme might be. Why do I always seem to have a bossy woman in my life? Why don't I trust men? Why am I scared of intimacy or that he/she will go off with somebody else? Why can't I keep a partner? Why can't I tell her what I feel? And so on. Looking at what happened to you in your childhood has become a powerful and useful therapeutic tool, but looking for the source further back in time reveals the root cause of the problem and gives you the opportunity to look at it from the perspective of your soul. As in the story of Ian and his brother in the previous chapter, it brings insight to a soulmate relationship that may not have been arrived at any other way.

But when the subject of past life exploration is mentioned to some people they reply with a 'No thanks! Got enough problems with this one without taking the lid off another can of worms!' If only they realised that today's problems and the way we experience them have their roots in the past and usually involve others who are from our soul group. Difficulties with relationships of any variety will always contain more information than initially meets the eye.

Belief in reincarnation has been around literally for ages. The ancient Egyptians, Hindus, Buddhists, Chinese Taoists, Jews, Greeks, Romans, Aboriginals, North American Indians, Theosophists, Sufis, Zoroastrians, Rosicrucians, Freemasons and no doubt a host of others believed that we have more than one crack at this experience we call 'life'. Past (and present) civilisations accepted rebirth as part of the evolution of the soul, and no wonder, since it is hardly likely that we would grasp what life in a human body was about in one short experience. Because we have been suffering from the spiritual amnesia mentioned in Chapter 1 for some time, most of us have forgotten who and what we really are. But now this is changing.

Accounts of people's past life experiences seemed only to appear in the twentieth century; presumably because the Church still held us all in the grip of its belief systems, which had written out all references to reincarnation from Christ's teachings, and influence from the east did not significantly percolate into our culture until the Beatles got involved with the Maharishi Mahesh yogi. The lid came off many things in the swinging sixties as the influence of the Aquarian Age began to impact. The windows were flung wide open to allow the wind of change to blow right through our personal and collective houses.

It seemed that many therapists kept quiet about their clients' past life recall, until the body of evidence could no longer be contained, and the work of many orthodox practitioners confirmed that an 'eruption of memory' was taking place. Gradually psychologists, doctors, psychiatrists and therapists have documented their clinical evidence and brought what was previously considered forbidden, irrational or just plain fantasy into the mainstream of current thinking. Is this another demonstration that the Age of Kali is coming to its conclusion, and history 'repeats itself'?

In my own work as a psychotherapist, the importance to people of exploring their personal archives became an imperative, as it seemed that entering an altered state of consciousness opened the door to a video library of memories that were linked to the presenting problem. For example, someone came to see me who had chronic eczema on both hands, which she had suffered since childhood. She spontaneously regressed to a lifetime in Nagasaki where she was a geisha girl, dressed in a beautiful satin dress and with a young daughter. As the atom bomb exploded, she looked down at her hands, which had started to melt. It was not the anguish attached to her death so much as the thought of what would befall her daughter that induced great distress in her. This was registered in her hands, and when she reincarnated some three or four years later that distress manifested as eczema. Several days after the session, she telephoned to say that the condition of her hands had vastly improved. By 'returning' to that traumatic past life experience, she had opened the complex of information buried in her subconscious mind, the symptoms of which had manifested themselves as eczema on her hands in this lifetime.

How does this work?

The Samskaras

As explained in Chapter 1, we are more than just a physical body. At death, the physical body and its etheric double separate from the upper complex of astral (or emotional), mental and soul bodies, and remain within the earth and its atmosphere, since they are made up of the same building blocks. Whatever we have considered as our 'selves' in this lifetime, the roles and dramas that we, as personalities, have been involved with, now shatter with the astral or emotional body – something like a jigsaw being thrown in the air. What then remains of this? Those moments of intense emotional experience, the times when we have been totally present, are taken with the soul. Most people spend most of their lives in a trance-like state. We do things without really knowing that we are doing them, and we talk without real purpose. If you think back on your life for a moment, how much of it can you really remember? So imagine this lifetime as a drama: you have acted out the full performance and now the play has ended. You put down the script entitled 'My Lifetime in the twenty-first Century' and go backstage to meet up with your fellow actors. This meeting takes place after the soul has travelled through the first stage of 'life' after life, known as the Bardo state, and is back home. Here the producer and the director, in the form of our council and spiritual elders, will be present to discuss the recent 'production'. There is no blame or judgement about the performance, simply compassionate wisdom and advice. But for you, or rather your soul, there may have been certain lines or moments in the play that made a 'mark' on you – somehow you just can't forget them.

These 'marks', in soul terms, are known as *samskaras*. They are literally 'scars' that the soul carries forward as unfinished business. They are emotional tracks inside our unconscious minds made by previous intense emotional experiences. A *samskara* is so indelibly marked on the mind and emotional body that it remains with the soul – something like a barnacle – on its journey into the inter-life state. These *samskaras* are brought in by the soul in its next or subsequent incarnations to be cleared. They are like packages of information hidden in the vast sea of the unconscious mind, but will be triggered by something external.

Mark, for example, came to see me for a past life re-gression. His 'problem' was that every time there was a Second World War film on television which contained scenes of the little planes flying over the Channel on recon-naissance or bombing raids, he would break down with uncontrollable grief. I asked him to remember one such film, and, as he closed his eyes, to imagine how he fitted into the scene. The memory was very close to the surface and he immediately said he was the pilot in the second plane; there were six of them on this mission. They were taken out of the sky by an enemy attack and plummeted into the sea. As he fell to his death his only thoughts were for his wife and two children whom he would no longer be able to support, and how much he loved them. He had 'let them down'. Of course it wasn't his fault that he was shot down in flames, but the emotions he felt at the point of death were so strong that they were taken by his soul to the interlife state. His wife was a soulmate in that life-time, and they were both working on the soul group's theme of abandonment and guilt. He recognised that in his present life he often felt over-responsible for those close to him, because he had not forgiven himself for leaving his wife and children to their fate in his last lifetime.

The first step in identifying our *samskaras* is to become aware of the clues that present themselves in our everyday lives, and to be able to differentiate between the re-actionary (as in action replay) energy of the *samskaras* and the *feelings* that come from our soul which, as explained in Chapter 1, are experienced as a sense of knowing. Everyday emotions are like the weather that exists in our personal atmosphere. Behind the clouds and rain, the sky of the soul is a constant blue. By identifying the nature of our *samskaras*, we can begin to stand back from them, and notice who and what it is that triggers their emotional response. Then we can be aware of the differ-ence between our astral body and our soul. Whenever you feel intense and often irrational emotions, as opposed to everyday ups and downs, you can be sure that the energy of a *samskara* is at work. Or you may find yourself with repetitive thoughts, which have no logical basis, particularly in soulmate relationships. 'I can't trust him,' even though he has never done anything to make you think he has or will betray you. 'All women are liars,' may be a mental script that was burned on the lips of a man leaving a previous incarnation, having been shocked to the core by the duplicity of some woman. He has brought it in with him again in order to release it, since it is not a truth. There will be a soulmate in female form in this lifetime who will evoke an echo of the past life situation, so that he can relive the experience in order to clear it and move on. Or repeat the circuit again.

Here are some of the characteristics of the *samskara*:

They make you feel de-centred, out of balance.

They cut you off from your environment, making you believe that you live in 'your' world as opposed to 'the' world.

They are re-actional, knee-jerk responses and can quickly turn into their opposite.

They cause a distorted view of reality as their waves of energy flow through your body.

They include the emotions of anger, jealousy, humiliation, shame, guilt and passionate possessive love.

They are triggered externally by people and situations.

They are based on control.

They cut you off and overshadow your soul by reinforcing your link to your astral or emotional body.

Whereas feelings of the soul are identified by the following:

They are unconditional – they do not need acknowledgement.
They are based on letting go and trusting that your soul knows what it is doing.
They make you feel centred.
They allow you to live in 'the' world, knowing that everything under the sun is connected to everything else.
They reinforce your connection to your soul which in turn widens your perspective.
Compassion, enthusiasm and a sense of just 'knowing' something.
They enhance your awareness.
They are stable, regardless of feedback.

Here is a soulmate story of Beverly, which demonstrates a *samskara* in action. She is an attractive, confident woman with two children and her own business. She used to enjoy seaside holidays with her children, but these were blighted by her sense of overwhelming panic when she was with them in the sea. Everything appeared to be fine – it was not a fear of the water itself – until she could not feel the ground under her feet, when she would become unnaturally distressed. She couldn't bear the feeling that her feet could not touch the bottom. She had another, more unusual prodding from this particular *samskara*, which was that her mouth seemed to produce quantities of water at night, when she slept. I asked her to close her eyes and imagine that she was in the sea with her children, and then had inadvertently got out of her depth; this evoked those feelings of panic, which was the link into the barnacle or *samskara*.

'When have you felt this feeling before?' I asked.

'Oh my God! I'm in the sea, it's dark . . . And I have got this beautiful dress on. I'm drowning – oh no!' She flails her arms and is in distress.

Once the link has been made from the external trigger to the internal complex of information, it is something like a video that comes up on the screen, except that you have the ability not only to be *in* the drama of the video, but your conscious, here-and-now mind is also present. The past life video can be rewound or fast-forwarded in order to collect the details of the story and to find what the important punctuation marks were in that lifetime.

'Go back to what has happened before you find yourself in the sea,' I say to her.

'I'm dancing with my fiancé on this wonderful boat; we are very much in love. Oh dear! We start to argue over some silly thing and I storm off the dance floor and go up on deck. Oh, it's rained and the boards are slippery. I've slipped and gone under the railings into the black sea. Oh God! They'll never find me; they don't even know that I have gone. He will think I don't love him, or deliberately taken my life – oh no!'

She becomes very distressed at this point, so I ask her to move through it quickly and to find herself hovering over the body that has just drowned.

'What are your thoughts and feelings?'

She says she feels a deep pain at the grief her fiancé will have suffered as a result of this. She berates herself for losing her temper, and saying things she didn't really mean. (In this lifetime, she never allows herself to get angry.)

I ask her to imagine her fiancé standing on the deck after the search for her body had been abandoned. Perhaps, although she is invisible now, she can make her 'presence' felt to him. Movingly, her anguish turns to a smile.

'I had a perfume he loved. He can smell it now . . . I am communicating to his mind: that we will meet again and I am so sorry.' This unspoken connection seems to bring some peace and solace to her fiancé, and although she does not want to leave him, the next step must be taken and she must return to her soul family. Once she had forgiven herself, the energy from the *samskara* is freed and there was no longer any fear of water.

As an increasing number of people are now able and interested in accessing their past life experiences, so the interlife state of consciousness, which is an integral part of this, will bring about changes that we can all look forward to. A past life regression is something like having a lucid dream; in other words a dream in which you are fully conscious and participating in. As your body relaxes, it allows your mind to move into an altered state. It is not hypnosis. This then allows the soul to bring forward an image – through the conduit of the right brain – like a frozen frame on a film strip. It is often extremely graphic and can contain sounds and smells. The 'story' attached to this frame then begins to unfold. It is the job of the therapist to ensure that the key events and people are identified and what the emotional punctuation marks and 'flavour' of that life are. The lifetime is 'worked' and then taken to the end and death of the physical body. Leaving the body and then looking down on it, and registering the thoughts and feelings about that incarnation produce a useful résumé, and the clues to what has been carried forward.

The Bardo: Balancing your Spiritual Bank Account

The next stage – the life-between-life state – is sometimes referred to as the Bardo, which in Tibetan literature means in-between. It is a waiting place between lifetimes, when one lifetime is finished and preparations are begun for another. It is experienced in a past life regression as something similar to a near-death experience. There is a sensation of leaving the body, looking down on it and then floating up to a higher realm where the soul now evaluates its experience on planet earth, and decides what experiences need to be gone through in its next incarnation. What issues need to be addressed and refined to bring about balance? The soul is not concerned with judging what is 'right' or 'wrong'. It is concerned only with bringing the polarities into balance to find equilibrium, where we know that we are souls having a human experience and can live, fully present in each moment, being the master of our minds, our bodies and our emotions.

This part of a past life regression experience can bring about a change in consciousness and often brings an almost overwhelming sense of compassion because here, beyond the confines of the physical body and out of time-bound reality, everything takes on a different perspective. Once we have left our physical body, leaving it like a friendly (or not, as the case may be) shell that we have been inhabiting for the duration of the 'life on earth' experience, we begin to feel the magnetic pull of a clear light that seems to draw us towards it. There is a sense of finally going home where we can understand the difficult and painful issues that might have plagued us on earth. For many people, this experience transforms their view of death and the mistaken notion that some kind of panel sits apportioning judgement. Questions such as, 'What are your thoughts and feelings about that life?' 'What is held in your body at the point of death?' or 'How is that character still active in you today?' and 'What advice would they give you in your current lifetime?' may be answered by the higher self without interference from the personality. Sometimes the soul has become so involved with the lifetime, or has died prematurely so that it is reluctant to leave and move to the next stage. For most people the passage to the interlife state feels like a liberation. The realisation that we are not confined to our bodies helps overcome the fear of death and brings clarity and understanding to relationships and situations.

The Karmic Boomerang

Another factor involved in the journey of the soul and its evolution in consciousness is the law of karma. Karma, translated from the Sanskrit, means 'action'. 'Whatsoever a man soweth, that shall he also reap,' said St Paul in his Epistle to the Galatians. The law of karma is a divine system of balance, counter-balance and perfect justice; a system in which nothing happens by accident. It is cause and effect simultaneously, because every action we take generates a force of energy that returns to us in kind, in the same way as a boomerang. It is the law used to justify inequalities and helps us understand why some people seem to get the book thrown at them and others sail through life. It is not a law of *punishment* for past actions, but a means by which the soul may experience both ends of a polarity, both ends of a pendulum swing, both sides of a coin.

'What have I done to deserve this?' cries the victim who feels that the finger of fate is continually punishing her. If only she could see that she is working with the theme of power (in this instance the lack of it). 'Why do women always betray me?' wails the man who has betrayed in previous lives. These questions become irrelevant when we understand that we, our selves (and at another level of consciousness) have orchestrated and worked with our karmic bank balance throughout all our lifetimes. As we are now in the throes of a major shift in consciousness on the earth it is time to move on from the trance-like hold the material world has over us. Instead of pointing our finger at fate or some other person when we struggle with our problems, we can raise our levels of awareness by recognising that what is happening to us is karma in action, asking us to look more deeply into the matter of being *in* the world but not of it. The soul itself requires the mirror of life to reflect back what adjustments need to be made, what cooking in the pot of life needs to be done. And who better to help us with this than a soulmate?

Understanding karmic law moves us from feeling like victims of life to empowerment; it also takes us beyond the judgement of others. How do we know what anyone else's soul is bringing forward for attention? Behind every abuser is the one who has been abused. When you look at the case histories of current child abusers, it generally reveals a background of a damaged or 'different' childhood. This is not to say that these acts should be condoned, but it helps to bring a wider, deeper perspective. Karma provides us with a kaleidoscope of opportunities to experience incarnation in a physical body. Over and over again, we play hero, villain, queen and slave and everything in between, gradually evolving through under-standing. We always have the free will and choice to shed those clothes that don't fit any more; the roles that we are tired of playing and which keep the pendulum of the theme we are working with swinging from one polarity to the other. We never take on in any one lifetime more than we can cope with. As Dr Elisabeth Kübler-Ross, author of *Living with Death and Dying*, says: 'you can take the pain and learn to accept it, not as a curse or punishment, but as a gift to you, a gift with a very specific purpose.'

A karmic soulmate will be one with whom there is un-finished soul business. The two lives were ended for what-ever reason in an inconclusive way. This is the strange story of Dorothy Eady, whose karmic soulmate had to wait over 3,000 years before he was able to put his karmic bank account with her in order. An English woman born in 1904, Dorothy fell down a flight of stairs in the home where she was the only child of Mr and Mrs Eady. She was three years old at the time, and was pronounced dead by the family doctor, who took her upstairs and put her on her bed until he could return with his nurse to wash and lay out the little body. However, he returned to find her sitting up and playing in her room. The death certificate he had prepared was torn up, and life apparently returned to normal.

But Dorothy began to have recurring dreams after this event. Dreams about a huge columned building with a beautiful surrounding garden. She also started to cry a lot, and when asked by her parents what was wrong, she would wail, 'I want to go *home*.' When she was four, her parents took her with them on a visit to the British Museum. She was bored with the whole proceeding until they entered the Egyptian section. Leaving her parents, she dashed from statue to statue, kissing their feet. She had to be forcibly removed when it was time to leave, kicking and screaming that she wanted to stay there: 'These are my people.'

A few months later her father bought her a copy of *The Children's Encyclopaedia* which, as luck would have it, contained photos and drawings of ancient Egypt. Dorothy would often be found poring over one particular page, peering through a magnifying glass to get more detail. The picture that fascinated her was of the Rosetta Stone. This is a huge piece of black basalt, discovered in 1799 in the Nile delta and inscribed with hieroglyphs, demotic symbols and fifty-four lines of Greek which provided the key to translation of the hieroglyphs for the first time. 'I know this writing,' she would say, 'but I have just forgotten it.'

By the time she was seven, she had begun to 'remember' what her dreams of the columned building were all about. Her father had brought home some magazines, and Dorothy had found among their pages a photograph of the Temple of Sety I at Abydos in Upper Egypt. Clutching this picture, she ran to her father. '*This* is my home! But why is it all broken, and where is the garden?' She then later came across another photograph that ran through her like a shock wave. It was of the well-preserved and lifelike mummy of Sety I, pharaoh of the Nineteenth Dynasty and builder of the temple at Abydos that featured in her dreams. 'I *know* him, I *know* him!' she informed her bewildered father.

'How can you *possibly* know him? He's been dead for three thousand years!'

It was in 1918, Dorothy by now fourteen, that she experienced the next 'milestone' on her journey to reunion with her ancient soulmate. She had gone to sleep reading a book about Egypt, as usual, and suddenly half awoke, feeling a weight on her chest. Then she saw a face, bending over her with both hands on the neck of her nightdress. Shock of shocks! It was the face of the mummy of Sety I, which terrified her, and yet she felt that something she had waited for had arrived at last. Then he tore her nightdress from neck to hem. She let out a cry, which brought her mother rushing in. 'How did you tear your nightdress for heaven's sake?'

'I must have done it myself,' Dorothy replied, knowing she couldn't possibly explain *this* to her mother. Later she would recount how she would never forget the look in his eyes which was 'of somebody in hell who had suddenly found a way out'.

After this she began to have a recurring dream which involved powerful images of herself as a young Egyptian girl called Bentreshyt (meaning 'Harp of Joy'), in this place she had now identified as Abydos. She would often find herself in a strange underground hall, part of the temple complex, where she was being beaten by a tall, frightening priest because she refused to answer his questions. This chamber that she found herself in was surrounded by water and had a floor covered with pebbles of agate, carnelian and turquoise. The young Dorothy Eady had no awareness of the fact that behind the Temple of Sety I in Abydos there is a strange and enigmatic structure known as the Osirian which has baffled Egyptologists and archaeologists alike, since it is clearly very much older than the temple itself. It has been constructed from huge blocks of sandstone, limestone and red granite, some of which weigh about 100 tons each. In the centre of the hall there is an island, surrounded by an artificial water channel, thought to represent the ancient mythical Island of Creation emerging from the primeval ocean. At age fourteen all this was confusing and disturbing for her to say the least, particularly the recurring experience of being interrogated by this tall, bald priest who would always end by beating her till she cried out, and then awoke.

Her passion for Egypt continued unabated, and when she was twenty-seven she went to London where she got a job with an Egyptian public relations magazine. Destiny led her to a meeting – at a debate in the House of Commons of all places – with Imam Abdel Meguid, an upper-middle-class Egyptian studying in London in order to become a teacher back in his homeland. They married and at twenty-nine Dorothy finally made preparations to return to the land of her dreams. During the second year of her marriage and now living in Cairo, she started to be 'visited' in the middle of certain nights by a gentleman who said his name was Hor-Ra. Dorothy would get out of bed in a state of semi-trance and go over to her desk where she would start writing. You can imagine how well received this was by her orthodox Muslim husband for whom it all became too much, and they finally divorced, but after Dorothy had given birth to a son who she named Sety of course.

The writings that came from the information that Hor-Ra was giving on his nocturnal visits helped her assemble the jigsaw of pieces she had collected over the years. It transpired that Bentreshyt (now Dorothy Eady) had been born of humble parents in Egypt around 1340 BC. Her mother died when she was two and her father then took her to the ancient temple at Kom el Sultan to be trained as a priestess. The high priest of this temple was a tall and frightening man called Antef. When Bentreshyt was twelve he asked her if she now wanted to go out into the world to find a husband, but since she knew nothing of life outside the temple and was happy there, she decided to stay. This meant she had to make a vow to remain a virgin and would become the property of the temple. It was at this time that the pharaoh Sety I was building his temple adjoining the Osirion at Abydos. He was a man in his fifties, and on one of his visits to Abydos to oversee construction work he happened to pass the gardens where he saw Bentreshyt gathering flowers. His Majesty, as she always referred to him, took the forbidden step of falling in love with this young temple virgin and together they 'ate the uncooked goose', the ancient Egyptian term for 'eating of the forbidden tree'. This act was considered a horrific breach of the religious laws of the time.

Sety was then called away to deal with trouble in Nubia and the gold mines of the Eastern Desert and little Bentreshyt's belly began to swell. When this news reached Antef's ears he tried to force her to confess her crime by beating the truth out of her with a stick. Finally she was coerced into revealing that it was the king who was the father of her child. 'This is a crime against Isis, of whom you are a priestess, and it is punishable by nothing less than death!' screeched the high priest. But by law the death sentence could not be passed without a fair trial and this would mean exposing His Majesty as the only man she had ever loved. Instead, she took her own life. When Sety returned to Abydos and asked about her, his heart broke at the news of her death. 'I will never forget her,' he vowed, and for 3,000 years he never did.

After Hor-Ra had told her the story of herself, which took him about a year, he departed, and visits from His Majesty began to take place. He told her that when he had died, he imagined he would find her in Amenti, the

Realm of the Dead, but after long years of suffering was told by the council that she was 'sleeping in the blackness and would one day be reborn'. Now he had found her.

Certain laws, it seems, still governed their relationship, even without their bodies. While Dorothy was still married, it was not appropriate for the union of these two souls to take place. However, once divorced, her astral body was free for total union with her beloved. Astral sex? One can only marvel at what kind of experience that might be! Dorothy also knew that these passionate etheric unions could not be continued once she returned to Abydos, as she knew she inevitably would. Once there, she was again 'temple property'. At fifty-two, she finally left Cairo and bought a one-way ticket to Abydos. When she eventually arrived at the temple, she described it 'as if I'd walked into a place where I'd lived before'. She knew where every-thing was, could read all the hieroglyphs and subsequently dedicated the remainder of her life until she died in 1981 to servicing the temple and healing people in the com-munity. Naturally she was considered to be pretty eccen-tric, to say the least, but she evoked a tremendous sense of devotion in those who knew her. Tourists coming to visit the remarkable temple of Sety I and the Osirian would find this woman, shoes left at the temple entrance, ready to explain the structure, the beautiful bas relief work, which is of exquisite quality, and the information contained in the copious hieroglyphs.

Sety continued to visit Dorothy when she was in Abydos, but their meetings were of a more consultative nature. This soulmate connection holds no questions of 'Is it . . . ?' or 'Isn't it . . . ?' and obviously brought great joy and relief to both parties even if it was somewhat unconventional.

She was called Omm Sety by the locals now, meaning that she was the mother (*ommi*) of Sety, her son. Living with her cats in a very simple mud brick house in Abydos, her days were spent at the temple. Her devotion did a lot to help restoration of this extraordinary sacred place to its original splendour.

A blow to the head, as experienced by Dorothy when she fell down the stairs, often precipitates an opening of the third eye chakra, which is linked to our memory banks. It is as if a knock to the head dislodges some shutter that prevents us from 'seeing' information that lies beyond the ring-pass-not of far memory. This can often be a traumatic experience as suddenly it seems as if the eyes and ears are capable of seeing and hearing more than the rest of us. No doubt our mental hospitals are full of people for whom this experience has been overwhelming and life-shattering, since it is no longer clear where 'reality' lies. Hence the importance, which cannot be understated, of 'grounding' or earthing yourself before exploring other realities. It is safe to travel anywhere once the link to home has been established. The signals from Dorothy Eady's past life were strong and unmistakable, although at that time she could easily have been diagnosed as suffering from some form of hallucinatory disorder. How might we know that we have been here before?

Clues to Who You May Have Been

Wanting to know who or what you might have been in a past life comes from a natural curiosity to discover more about ourselves, and the benefits are many if your regression is facilitated by a qualified practitioner. It might be interesting, but is of little real value to be told by someone else that you have been a Tibetan monk or Egyptian princess. This is not going to help you do your laundry. You need to know for yourself, and this knowing comes from the experience. If you have been wondering what past lives you may have lived, there are other clues as well as the re-actionary emotional stuff that the *samskaras* continue to bring to our notice. The guide to whether you have a positive or uncomfortable response to any of the following triggers will be the clue to what sort of a life you might have led in that past time-frame. It's important to point out that not all karma is negative. We have not always been suffering, tortured and badly behaved human beings who spend the rest of our lifetimes reaping the effects of a painful karmic boomerang. We can create positive karma – thank goodness. What goes around can come around in a positive and beneficial way if we have put acts of compassion, unselfishness and humility into our soul's 'bank account'. But there is a world of difference, of course, between a compassionate act that comes from the heart, and one that is done for the purpose of acknowledgement. Truly unselfish acts are often the ones that go unsung and unseen on earth.

Some of the many clues to lives lived elsewhere and in different bodies may include:

An inexplicable draw to a different culture, language or country. The converse of this may be 'I have *never* wanted to go to Australia – I don't know why.'

The games you enjoyed playing as a child.

Particular plays, films or books, period dramas, or characters in any of those.

77

Fears or phobias which may be of rats, snakes, heights, enclosed spaces, water, fire, relationships, having children, obsessive compulsive disorders.

Physical disabilities, lumps, bumps, birthmarks or other physical anomalies.

Illogical mental scripts such as 'Don't trust anyone' or 'I'll never have enough.'

And of course, other people to whom we may take an instant dislike, or feel as if we have known 'for ever' – our soulmates.

Anything, in fact, that doesn't make logical sense or cannot be linked to an event in this lifetime. In summary, your past lives will inevitably have soulmates woven into them because life on earth without relationships is not a life fully lived even though you may have had the experience of a life spent in solitude, if that is part of your theme. Our souls are forever pulling us back towards love, as our egos drive us in other directions. Opening our personal history books helps us all to see and remove the obstacles to living life on earth more lovingly, compassionately and respectfully. But we are creatures of habit who don't much like change. Soulmates will see to it that we do – for better or for worse; that's their job and you signed the agreement with them. There's no escape from the lessons that need to be learned, I'm afraid. Your soul sets off for its earthly sojourn with its agenda for life and the items on this agenda are encoded into our human systems, otherwise how would we get on with our specific purpose? It has been extremely well organised, when you think about it. This information needs to be made 'active' and the activation is a key role played by our soulmates.

4

the chakras

Microchips of Soul Information

These flowers are the sense organs of the soul.
RUDOLF STEINER

So, at this point in earth time, most of us have forgotten who we are, where we came from and don't really know what we're doing here. We are somehow magnetically drawn to the words soul and soulmate, which have made a comeback in our culture, but we have little notion of what they really mean.

You may by now begin to get the feeling that you are more than you thought you were. Your anatomy includes aspects (on the outside!) that you can't see, and your history goes back into the mists of time. You are here for a reason – a purpose – and you've picked up this book because you want to know more about soulmates.

Soulmates may not give us the happily ever after experience, but they will polish the lantern of your soul. They will push your buttons, drive you mad, frustrate, entrance, infuriate and possibly sometimes love you. They may bully, abuse, reject, ignore or humiliate. They may be needy, take you into speechless grief or jealousy, but you will notice them.

The *samskaras* will resonate with external triggers to give us clues as to where the source of our fears, phobias and illogical reactions lies. The law of karma will see to it that we reap what we sow, and there is also a factory-installed system within us containing 'microchips' of soul information that will ensure that the issues we need to look at are encoded into our human personality.

These microchips are called 'chakras' and are keys to unlocking the soul's secrets. Chakra is a Sanskrit word meaning 'wheel', and describes what they would look like if we could see them with the naked eye. They are referred to in the east as lotus flowers, each one having a different number of petals. The root chakra has four, for example, while the crown is the 'thousand-petalled lotus'. They are in fact funnel-shaped, spinning energy vortices, which interface with your physical body and your subtle or 'unseen' anatomy. These invisible 'wheels' link your physical body and auric field and are junction boxes on an invisible circulatory grid system whose interconnecting lines and pathways are known as 'meridians'. The points of intersection are known as *nadis* and it is this web of energy lines that is used by acupuncturists.

The chakras are the seven major energy sources on this energetic grid, spinning vital life force, known as *prana* or *chi*, out to the extremities of our physical being. They are step-down transformers for the intake of vital life force, without which we would cease to exist, since it is used by the hormonal, nervous and cellular systems of our physical body. They function as a system and are affected by the health of the body and our emotional 'weather'.

As we have seen, the soul, with the counsel of others in its group and guidance from those that 'oversee' the soul's evolution, decides what circumstances will offer the best opportunities for growth and understanding. Which culture, geographical location, parents and soulmates will provide us with the situations required to bring us to the realisation of who we really are. It then leaves home, calibrating and constellating its energy to enter the tiny physical form that will be its vehicle for the next incarnation. It enters through the crown chakra at the top of the head, which is open to receive it and evident in the fontanel in babies. Even though the plates of the cranium come together as we grow up, this place of entry is our connection to where we came from and will never completely close no matter what life throws at us and how 'disconnected' we may become later on. The other chakra that is open is the root, since we need to engage with our physical bodies, or nothing much will happen. All the other chakras are like little buds on the stem of a flower which will open as we develop into adults, and their opening and healthy flowering will depend on what experiences we encounter and how we are affected by these experiences.

Since the purpose of the soul's journey on earth is to clear its karmic backlog and release the *samskaras*, and we have gone through the ring-pass-not of forgetfulness, how on earth do we remember what we are here to do? That information is encoded into the chakras. Our biology is indeed our biography, but it is not always obvious until we understand the clues, until our buttons are pressed.

We need our difficult soulmates to push these buttons, to bring up the unfinished business of the soul. *Which* of these buttons is being pressed will send a clear message from your soul about the issues that need to be addressed in this lifetime (and however many more, before you wake up to what your soul is trying to communicate to you).

Luckily not all of these seven buttons are waiting to be pressed. It may be that the feelings hidden behind only one of them are so sensitive that you have unconsciously put them in a lead-lined box and wrapped them up in barbed wire so no one can get anywhere near them. Enter a soulmate, with wire cutters and blowtorch to reveal the treasure locked away inside.

With the death of the western alchemical tradition, when mind, body and soul were separated into three different compartments, we exchanged our alchemical skills and esoteric knowledge in favour of a mechanistic view of the world and all it contained. It was not so in the east, where Hindus and Taoists did not sell out to the Cartesian notion that the world was an entropic machine moving from Big Bang to Big Crunch. The science that we have set so much store by now states, thanks to quantum physics, that actually the universe is like an expanding flower after all.

In these 'enlightened' days, esoteric knowledge has left the confines of the mystery schools and the monasteries and can be found on the bookshelves of every town in the land. Reading about my auric field and chakra system, however, does not give me the understanding of what they are and how they work. Direct experience is the only way truly to *know*. Our interest here lies in what they have to do with soulmates. Since there are many excellent works already written on the subject of chakras in general, I will narrow the information down to their specific button-pressing qualities, but first a few basic chakra facts.

Each one has:

A direct connection with a nerve plexus, an endocrine gland and an important body system – excretory, reproductive, digestive, circulatory, respiratory and cognitive – and thus are directly implicated with the health of the body.

An association with a specific colour, which reflects their rate of vibration. The red of the root chakra, for example, spins slower than the amethyst of the crown.

A correspondence with a different physical, emotional and spiritual issue.

A specific button that may be pushed by a soulmate in order to bring an issue, which has been carried forward from a previous incarnation, to our attention.

The capacity to be over- or under-active according to the specific thoughts and feelings that affect it.

A different age at which they develop or 'open'.

Going through the chakras one by one is like inspecting the instruments in an orchestra. They operate as a whole system under the direction of the conductor, the third eye chakra. The conductor did not write the symphony nor can he play every instrument, but he needs to know what the composer (the soul) had in mind and how best to express the essence of the music. He needs to know if the flautist has flu or the percussionist a tendency to go over the top because of family problems.

Just like a small orchestra, the health of each player is vital to the harmony of the whole. Our individual chakras may get out of balance and can be over- or under-active, thus affecting the whole system. If this situation endures, eventually the physical body will be affected. Another indicator, therefore, that there is work to be done and issues to be addressed, will be the body itself expressing its dis-ease at the thoughts or feelings that are affecting that chakra. Those with continuous throat problems need to ask themselves what it might be that they are not saying, not expressing. Heartache is not the physical heart weeping, but the energy of the heart chakra coming into focus. Digestive problems will tell us that the solar plexus chakra is struggling with issues of power and control, and so on.

The seven major players in the chakra orchestra that, when playing in harmony, will sound your own very particular note are the root, the sacral, solar plexus, heart, throat, third eye and crown. As you go through the information on each chakra, ask yourself which of your energy centres is being affected by a soulmate.

The BASE or ROOT Chakra: *Colour – RED*

This, as its name suggests, has to do with feeling safe in your body, being fully present in the physical world, and 'earthed'. All electrical gadgets need to be earthed and we are no exception. If, from the moment we were born, we never felt safe, a soulmate will challenge us to stand our ground, be in our bodies and not in our own little world. They will push us to get in touch with our earthiness. If you have a need to mother, or be mothered, or you feel like a needy child and want a soulmate to make you feel safe, this chakra and its history must be investigated so that you can stand on your own two feet. The other side of this coin is an over-identification with the material world, a 'jungle' mentality that gives no thought for anything above the belt.

Position on the body:	Perineum (central point between the legs).
Relates to:	Feet, legs, lower abdomen and its contents.
Body speaks through:	Constipation, IBS, colitis, piles, problems with the rectum, hips, legs and feet.
Thoughts that affect:	It's not safe to be here. I can't stand my ground. I don't belong. I might not survive. I'll never have enough.
Feelings that affect:	Not in the body. Not really 'here'. Disconnection. Fear of the earthy side of life.
Past life themes:	Physical or emotional trauma which makes it unsafe to fully engage with the body in this incarnation. Lives of physical deprivation, starvation, suffering and insecurity.

Questions for the Root Chakra

Why did I choose these parents and this culture?

What might my mother have been feeling when she was carrying me?

How was I received?

How were the first two or three years of my life?

What do I feel about my body? Is it safe to be in it?

Do I really want to be here?

> *A soulmate will push our buttons concerning:*
> Security   Safety   Stability
> Body consciousness   A sense of 'belonging'

The SACRAL or WATER/SEXUAL Chakra: Colour – ORANGE

This chakra and its secrets will be of particular interest to anyone whose soulmate triggers issues concerning sexuality and intimacy. Since our sexuality is the creative life force itself, it should not spend its life locked away. On the other hand over-indulgence and casual sex lead to another sort of imbalance, since this violates the sacredness of two bodies fused in union. It's about intimacy and pleasure, as well, and not necessarily only in a sexual context. The effect a soulmate will have on this chakra may be to help you take off your 'hair shirt' if you've got one on, and to stop feeling guilty if you enjoy yourself. Conversely, it may be time to take your sexuality and creativity more seriously. It may be that you and your soulmate have to face the inability to produce children, or consider abortion, and then deal with the emotions that this brings up. If you have no sexual partner, or have chosen to be celibate at least for a time, it does not mean you can forget about this chakra. A soulmate in this case will challenge your creative expression in other ways: your music, your writing, your business plan, your choice of clothes.

Position on the body:	Just below the navel/the sacrum.
Relates to:	Reproductive and urinary systems.
Body speaks through:	Cystitis, prostatitis, nephritis, menstrual difficulties and sexual dysfunction.
Thoughts that affect:	I dare not be intimate. Mustn't get too close. I can't cope with change. Sex is everything. Sexual feelings are 'wrong'.
Feelings that affect:	Resistance to change. Repression of sexuality. Denial of creativity in its widest sense. Lack of self-respect. Guilt at pleasurable feelings.

Past life themes: Lifetimes when sexuality ended in terminal disaster: persecution, betrayal, guilt. Lives as religious celibates in denial of sexuality. Lives when creativity, following your dream, led to despair or death, or when your sexual drive led you to acts that were deeply regretted. Lives where there were illegal abortions, unwanted children or death in childbirth.

Questions for the Sacral Chakra

What were my parent's attitudes to intimacy and pleasure?

How do I feel about my own sexuality?

If I take myself back to the age of three, four or five, what did I love doing?

How do I express my creativity now?

How do I manage change?

What has been the most important relationship in the whole of my life?

A soulmate will push our buttons concerning:
Intimacy   Sexuality   Flexibility
Creativity   Spontaneity

The SOLAR PLEXUS Chakra: Colour – YELLOW

This is the home of our will and determination. It is sometimes referred to as our 'emotional mind'. Just about everyone, unless they are emotionally dead, will be aware of their solar plexus chakra, since it gives us 'butterflies', gut feelings and can be knocked for six by an emotional shock. It is our power base, and is therefore deeply involved in issues of control. It's the key to understanding the soul themes of master/slave, bully/victim, and will certainly be a popular soulmate button, since most of us are working to a greater or lesser degree with these archetypes. Who's the boss? Can we give out without giving in? Do we have to be *right*, or bend over backwards to be liked? The lower three chakras, root, sacral and solar plexus, are concerned with issues of life on earth. Since our past experiences as souls in bodies haven't always been much of a laughing matter, these three will almost certainly need attention. Soulmates are doing their utmost for each other to unblock the energy here, so that it can move up to the next level of expression.

Position on the body:	Solar plexus.
Relates to:	Digestive system, pancreas, liver, the ego.
Body speaks through:	Ulcers, eating disorders, diabetes, hypertension, disorders of the stomach, pancreas, gall bladder, liver.
Thoughts that affect:	I've got no drive, I can't do it. He makes me feel small. I am better than her. I'll do what they tell me. I'm always right.
Feelings that affect:	Fear of authority figures. Shame. Rage and aggression, Arrogance. Low self-esteem.
Past life themes:	Use and abuse of power over others – master/slave dramas. Lifetimes when it was not safe to be yourself, when you had to bend yourself out of shape or face the consequences. Lives as victims, or alternatively, power freaks ('If I am not in control, I will be controlled').

Questions for the Solar Plexus Chakra

What situations make me feel threatened?

Do I give away power to avoid confrontation?

Am I afraid of my own power?

Do I want to get my own way?

What would happen if I lost control?

How do I respond to emotions?

A soulmate will push our buttons concerning:
Personal power   Equality
Will

The HEART Chakra: Colour – GREEN/PINK

Ah . . . we have arrived at the heart, the centre of the system in more ways than one. The opening of our hearts is the goal of every single soulmate encounter. When we 'come from the heart' we can rise above the issues of security (root), sexuality (sacral) and personal power (solar plexus) – they will fall away in the face of a force so powerful that they cease to exist in their old forms. That force is love. Not any old love, but the kind that has no strings attached, no conditions, no scripts and hidden agendas. The heart is for giving and forgiving. A painful soulmate encounter will be asking us to transcend the judgement of right or wrong, rejection, abandonment and grief and feel the power of compassion – *whatever* they have done to us. Since no doubt we have done the same thing to them in a previous lifetime, isn't it time for the heart to put a stop to tit-for-tat karma? The heart is the seat of the soul, as civilisations throughout time have known. It's

89

the interface between heaven and earth, and our arms are its outreach, bringing us together, heart to heart, in a hug. Love radiates, it expands, it changes the rate of vibration of our whole aura and it's in urgent need of polishing at this moment in our history. When our hearts step into the driving seats of our lives, miracles begin to happen. Who is the soulmate who is the hardest to love, the most difficult to forgive, the most painful to think of? They are waving a key in our faces to the most important doorway to our soul.

Position on the body:	Centre of the chest, to the right of physical heart.
Relates to:	Cardiovascular and autoimmune system.
Body speaks through:	Heart and circulatory problems, cancer, AIDS, ME and allergies.
Thoughts that affect:	Love is difficult. I can't love myself. I love too much. No one loves me. I can't forgive them/myself. I feel vulnerable. I might get hurt.
Feelings that affect:	Love. Grief. Courage. Compassion. Empathy. Yearning. Bitterness.
Past life themes:	Times when the heart was broken by grief or pain resulting in 'It's not safe to love'. Times when vulnerability and openness led to an overwhelming experience (betrayal, loss, separation, unrequited love). A lifetime where you left your body with the *samskara* of 'I will never forgive them/myself because of what has happened.'

Questions for the Heart Chakra

What makes you sing?

Who gave you love without strings attached?

If you are closed and defended, what do you need? What are you afraid of?

Is forgiveness of myself or another needed?

Can you remember joy?

What stops me from telling someone that I love them when I'm uncertain of their response?

A soulmate will push our buttons concerning:
Love without strings and conditions
Forgiveness   Grief   Courage   Vulnerability
Giving/receiving love   Compassion

The THROAT Chakra: Colour – TURQUOISE/AQUAMARINE

The throat chakra is all about communication – honest communication. It's about self-expression. Our voices say a lot about the people we are and the state of the other chakras in our orchestras. A soulmate helping you to free this chakra may paralyse you into speechlessness so that you literally lose your voice, or you may find yourself babbling because somehow a silence between you feels threatening. Perhaps your soulmate makes you shout and scream, releasing torrents of verbal lava that you regret later on. Or perhaps you are on the receiving end of cutting comments that seem to shrivel and hurt you. Where's your voice? Open your mouth, says your soul, and trust *me* to speak your truth, not the truth of the solar plexus and all its problems with power and control, but the truth of your soul. By checking with whom you can and cannot express yourself freely and clearly (and why that is) you will discover who it really is who speaks for you.

Position on the body:	Neck, throat, mouth, nose and ears.
Relates to:	Upper respiratory tract, thyroid, organs of speech.
Body speaks through:	Problems in neck, throat, mouth and gums. Sinuses, nasal congestion, over/under-active thyroid.
Thoughts that affect:	Mustn't say anything. Better keep quiet/fill the silence with words. Don't trust myself. What will they think if I say that? Can't express myself.
Feelings that affect:	Fear. Worthlessness. Trust.
Past life themes:	Lives when opening your mouth resulted in disaster. Lives as preachers or someone with a 'message' who died for broadcasting their beliefs. Lives involved with secrets and lies and their consequences.

Questions for the Throat Chakra

Do I always say what I mean and mean what I say?
Do I feel uncomfortable with silence?
If I let people know who I really am, will I be accepted?
If I say what I feel, will I hurt others? Do I care?

A soulmate will push our buttons concerning:
**Speaking the truth   Trust   Communication
Self-expression**

The BROW Chakra or THIRD EYE: Colour – Indigo Blue

The third eye is so called because it represents the 'inner' eye that sees in all directions. It is the seat of our intuition and inner vision and functions when the left and right hemispheres of the brain are in synchrony. It is sometimes referred to as the Gateway to the Void. It is the home of our imagination and channel for our dreams and other communications from our soul. This eye that you can't see is the vital tool for experiencing and exploring the inner passageways of the self. A soulmate (because they are scared) may try to rubbish your insights and intuitive hunches, thus undermining your psychic gifts. This chakra will also be affected by a soulmate who plays mind games with you (or you with them), thereby disempowering your own ability to 'see' for yourself. There are many charlatans around who take advantage of those who don't believe they have their own psychic abilities. The challenges of this chakra are about opening your visionary abilities, which we all have.

Position on the body:	Above and between the eyebrows.
Relates to:	Mind, brain, eyes.
Body speaks through:	Tension headaches, migraine, visual problems.
Thoughts that affect:	It's only my imagination. I don't trust my intuition. Logic is the only way to sort things out. Dreams are rubbish.
Feelings that affect:	Confusion. Clarity of vision.
Past life themes:	Lifetimes as witches, magicians and seers when the use of insight, intuition and inner

vision ended in death or persecution. Abuse
of magical powers.

Questions for the Third Eye Chakra

Do I trust my intuition?
Do I pay attention to my dreams?
What inner visions do I have?
Do I take a balanced view of life?

A soulmate will push our buttons concerning:
Insights   Intuition   Our psychic abilities,
dreams and vision
Lack of logic and its opposite

The CROWN Chakra: Colours – AMETHYST/SILVER/WHITE/GOLD

The crown chakra is the direct link to your soul and its
family and the higher spiritual realms. It is your connection
to the divine source. A halo around someone's head will
tell you about the strength of their soul presence. A soulmate may appear in your life in the form of a guru or spiritual 'master' if your connection needs to be worked on,
because no master or guru can give you what your soul
seeks for itself. Because of the importance of this chakra to
the soul, a soulmate connection affecting it will be heavy-
duty. You may be so adversely affected by them that there
seems to be no point in living at all. This may be because
they die or leave, or it may be (as in my own story) that it
feels as if they have captured your very soul. This makes
you feel that your connections to the outside world and

more especially your divine purpose have been severed. The challenge here is to realise that *nothing* and *no one* can take away that divinity within you, and this soulmate has actually taken you into the deepest part of your well of loneliness and separation – a dark night of the soul. This can prove to be a major turning point since a cry of help from the depth of your being is always heard by the soul's invisible supporters. It is through the crown chakra that we become aware of our unity with all things: beautiful music, being in nature, the look in a baby's eyes or whatever it is that makes you lose yourself into a wider experience.

Position on the Body:	Top of the head.
Relates to:	Top of the Skull.
Body speaks through:	Depression, epilepsy, nerve/brain and mental disorders.
Thoughts that affect:	Life is pointless. There is no higher power – I don't believe in anything.
Feelings that affect:	Despair. Desolation. Isolation. Futility. Connection. Sense of purpose.
Past life themes:	Lifetimes when you felt your god had deserted you. Lives when religious fervour had an adverse affect on you. Lives as martyrs, saints or holy people – or destroyers of such people.

Questions for the Crown Chakra

Who am I?
What am I doing here?
Am I alone?
Is there a god?

> A soulmate will push our buttons concerning:
> Our religious and spiritual views
> Our connection to our soul

This chapter will have helped you identify what a soul-mate is pushing you to look at. If it all feels like hard work then you are going for the soft option, nothing will change and your patterns will go on repeating until, either in this life or the next, you will decide to pull yourself out of your apathy and make a move towards the next step on your journey. It's not about looking for trouble, but if you have picked up this book, then your soul is suggesting that NOW is the time for change, not tomorrow or next week. It is, after all, about living life more fully, without fear, and expressing your true nature.

The next chapter, on the shadow, will take you deeper into your understanding of your self, and however diffi-cult, soulmate relationships are the guides and dragons that show us the way and guard the pearls in the oysters of our soul.

Every part of the body has a story to tell.
ANNA HALPRIN

the power of
the shadow
Working in the Dark

One does not become enlightened by imagining figures of light,
But by making the darkness conscious.
C.G. JUNG

It is only when the sun is directly overhead that it casts
no shadow. Only when we are completely aligned with
the source, in a state of balance, will our shadow disappear. Until such time, our shadow dances around us,
catching our attention and daring us to peer into the dark
side of our nature. Since we are not sure of what might
lurk in the deep, dark aspects of ourselves, we prefer not
to look in this direction, and will turn away, putting a
mask over the face we would rather not see or have seen.
We run from our shadow, and avoid looking it in the eye
through workaholism, mind-numbing television, Prozac,
alcohol, sex, food or mood-altering drugs. We may become
ill, or we may sink into depression and resort to chem-
icals which prevent the waves of despair from totally
flooding our being.

We all have a shadow, and until we are aware of at

least some of its content, a major part of our energy will be unavailable to us. Our subconscious mind requires energy to contain our shadow, in order to keep it locked away from painful scrutiny. Soulmates who help us reveal the shady sides of ourselves will definitely not be of the feather duster variety. They are more likely to be sewage inspectors and dynorods – and no one likes having the contents of their blocked drains exposed.

Robert Bly, the gifted contemporary poet and thinker, describes the shadow thus:

> *We spend our life until we're thirty deciding what parts of ourselves to stuff into the invisible bag we drag behind us, and we spend the rest of our lives trying to get them out again.*

As children we enter the world pure, innocent and spontaneous balls of energy. But there's work to do, and so before too long we begin to realise that some of the feelings that we have are not acceptable to those on whom we rely for love and survival. There will certainly be one or more soulmate in your family or peer group who are responsible for activating your soul theme. The feelings that they bring up in you are too much to cope with, too painful to realise, so they get pushed down into the unconscious shadow basement of your self and locked away.

'Don't do that – it's dirty,' and sexual feelings get put in the bag.

'If you don't stop crying, I'll smack you,' and tears get stuffed into the bag.

'You mustn't hurt your sister,' and aggression joins the

others, along with shame, rage, powerlessness, creativity (don't make a mess), chaos, laughter and a host of other feelings that we perceive to be unacceptable or inappropriate. We learn to cope by developing 'strategies' in childhood that will create adult people-pleasers, caretakers, victims (poor me!), workaholics, controllers and people who are cut off from their feelings.

Our chakras, like little time bombs, are encoded with the information that will need to come to the surface in this incarnation, but it needs to be 'activated'.

By the time we are teenagers, we're already dragging a sack of potatoes. Now we need the approval of our peers, and more 'unacceptable' traits go into our bag. It takes a strength and determination to hold on to one's true nature in the face of these cultural and tribal pressures that most of us do not have at that time in our lives. We are sculpted, shaped and shaved so that by the time we are in our twenties, there is more of us in the bag than out of it.

All this goes on unconsciously, so it is as if we are living our lives on the tiny visible part of a huge iceberg, most of which is hidden in the sea beneath us. If you are feeling threatened, or denying that this applies to you, then just spend a moment reflecting on what it was 'inappropriate' to express when you were young. What aspects of yourself were pared away and buried out of sight? How did you have to behave in order to get the love and attention that is as fundamental to a child as food and water? What feelings were unacceptable in your family, and to whom?

Closely scrutinising our early lives will tell us what parts of us lie mute in their coffins, and the key that unlocks the door to the cellars and basements of our being will be found in recognising the soulmates who initially seemed to be responsible for the difficult experiences of our early years. They may not have *intended* to hurt us, but that's what happened. Like Ann, whose soul is working with the theme of trust. When she was five, her elder sister (a soulmate) told her, 'Don't be so silly – of course there isn't a Father Christmas. It's Daddy!' From that moment on, she lost her ability to trust what people told her and disbelief became the safer option. She had 'forgotten' this incident until her relationship with her partner hit a crisis because she could not trust that he was telling her the truth. In regression therapy she brought that past event out into the open, enabling her to realise that her mistrust belonged to the little girl who felt she had been betrayed. This story had its roots in past lives when taking someone's word had led to more radical consequences.

These experiences will often (but not always) be linked to our past lives. Issues concerning power or the lack of it in the past will drop us into a family where we easily lose our own sense of self. Or if we are working on the theme of abandonment, for example, we may find ourselves as an adopted child in this lifetime trying to cope with the feeling that 'nobody wants me' – a feeling too painful to go into, so it gets locked away. But the energy of that unacceptable feeling runs like an undercurrent through that person's life until it is recognised and a natural flow restored.

The problem with these feelings that get stuffed away is that they may be dead, or more accurately numbed out, but they do not lie down. There comes a moment in most people's lives – and very often this comes as a crisis in mid-life – when the energy required to contain and restrain the contents of our shadow can no longer keep the lid on things and, like a pressure cooker, a head of steam builds up which may finally explode and put stew all over the ceiling. In this case, rabbit stew . . .

I will never forget Dr Elisabeth Kübler-Ross, at one of her powerful Life, Death and Transition workshops, telling of her own shadow experience. Elisabeth was an identical twin, born of a stern Swiss psychiatrist and his wife. It was difficult for people to differentiate between the two girls, except that Elisabeth was the one who kept rabbits. She kept this little family of hers out in the stables and had come to terms with the fact that every so often her father would select one of them to go into the pot for Sunday lunch. But she had a favourite – Blacky – who she used to cover with straw so her father could not see him when he carried out his grim selection. Of course the dreaded day came when Blacky was spotted. Her father pointed at the rabbit and said, 'This one, Elisabeth, today.' She then had to take her little friend along to the butcher, carry back his warm remains and then – oh, horror of horrors – sit at the table with Blacky in the pot. No tears, no remonstrations – they were unacceptable in that family. Her pain doesn't bear thinking about.

It was not until she was in her fifties, getting her luggage checked in at an airport, that the lid was taken off the feelings she had held down and 'forgotten' about for so long. An official pointed at one of her suitcases: 'This one, please.' And all the grief, impotence and rage of the little seven-year-old flooded her system. As she said, 'I lost it then and there in the airport. I was uncontrollable and inconsolable.' She explained that when she finally calmed down, she realised that it now felt as if she had put down a heavy load which she wasn't even aware that she had been carrying. The feelings held in Elisabeth's shadow were released in a rush, triggered by the memory of what a pointing finger had created for her in her childhood. Perhaps in a past life it was not a rabbit, but a loved one who she had had to see executed, and this was the echo of that situation in the current incarnation.

The trouble is we all want to be perfect, kind, compassionate and loving people, but unfortunately this is not the case. Denial of the existence of our shadows will result in persistent reminders in the form of repeating patterns of behaviour or continually finding people in our lives who press the same old button. Sometimes the pressure in the shadow builds up to the point where we fall apart. This is the break-up to break through, which we have called a 'breakdown'. It appears in these moments as if our world has totally collapsed and our connections to everyone and everything seem to be severed. It is often the job of a soulmate to precipitate this moment of truth in your life.

The Darkest Hour is Before the Dawn

Because of its depth of feeling, an emotional crisis of any magnitude is often referred to as a 'dark night of the soul' but it is in reality an enormous step on the path of becoming who we really are. 'Dark night of the soul' is a phrase first used in a poem written by the Spanish mystic, St John of the Cross, who in 1578 wrote 'Songs of the Soul Which Rejoice at Having Reached . . . Union with God by the Road of Spiritual Negation', which is a sixteenth-century way of saying he went through a breakdown to find union with the divine.

St John of the Cross experienced his dark night of the

soul when imprisoned for his beliefs in a tiny windowless prison cell in Toledo. His only excursions were occasional visits to the refectory where he was publicly scourged by his jailers. All were astonished by his meek acceptance of his fate. Why did he not defend himself? He waited patiently for the divine answer that would end this hell on earth. Deprived of his freedom, all he had was his connection to his divine self. No one can become a saint without solving the problem of suffering, says Thomas Merton in his essay on St John of the Cross. It is a *living* solution, burned in the flesh and spirit of the saint by fire. So the soulmate(s) of St John were those who persecuted him, thus facilitating the opportunity for the deepest of all soul experiences on earth: an experience that broke something open within him and gave him a mystical experience that is beyond words.

> As silver is tried by fire, and gold in the furnace, so the Lord trieth hearts.
>
> PROVERBS 17, 3

For lesser, more ordinary mortals such as ourselves, the process is somewhat similar in that a dark night of the soul strips us of everything that we have relied upon to give us our 'identity'. We are reduced to nothing or at least nothing in the eyes of our egos. Anyone on a spiritual journey will go through this experience to a greater or lesser degree, but it is not, mercifully, usually as radical as St John's experience. For some, the contents of the shadow bag may be 'drip fed', or rather 'drip released' through therapy or other ways of self-realisation depending on whether you have contracted at a soul level to take your medicine all at once, or over a period of time. Not everyone, thankfully, has elected to take the dark night fast track.

Someone like Pat, for example, who is a sensitive woman from an ordinary, loving family but one where demonstrations of feelings were not allowed. 'Shows of emotion' were so unacceptable that her mother would never go to a funeral for fear that she would shed a tear (and release the floodgates of her lifetime). Pat's adult soulmate relationships involved men who were so emotionally absent they may as well have been on another planet. She married a brilliantly creative man who never once told her that he loved her. Little by little, the pressure from her feelings that had been shut up for so long began to push themselves to the surface, until she finally walked out of her marriage (and job) she'd held on to for twenty years. She left to follow her heart's desire to become a painter.

Her feelings, now out of the shadows, drew Michael towards her, and another area of passionate expression was opened up. Unfortunately he decided to marry someone else, leaving her to deal with pain and loss and to sweep up the pieces of her life. She found her way to a therapist who gently helped her look at the contents of her shadow bag and to bring them into the light of understanding. She made friends with her feelings, instead of locking them all up again through fear. She could see that the patterns of hiding her feelings – initiated in childhood – had manifested themselves in the mirror of her adult relationships. Michael had opened the door of her heart not only to passion and love, but also to the other side of the coin: grief and loss. Perhaps the torrent of tears she released then were also expressed on behalf of her mother. She has made the journey (with the help of her soulmates) to her self. She can see the stages that led from her emotionally distant parents, through her absent partners to the breaking open of her heart, revealing feelings she didn't know existed. She has no partner at the moment, preferring to become more familiar with her new way of being in the world.

The ancient Egyptians, in their wisdom, knew about the presence of our shadow. In their mystery schools the feelings buried in our subconscious were known as 'Obstacles to Flight': constellations of stuck energy that prevented the upward flight of consciousness. Releasing them was an initiatory process. Initiations are all about crossing the threshold from the mundane to the sacred, and those who were to become privy to the eternal mysteries had to go through a series of initiations in the temples along the Nile – each one a different test – before qualifying for the final initiation in the Great Pyramid. Here in the so-called Pit, deep beneath the pyramid itself, initiates would have whatever fears they might still be holding amplified so that they could recognise any remaining obstacles to the flight of their soul.

This descent into darkness is relevant here, in our study of soulmate connections, because it will often involve a soulmate, acting like an Egyptian priest and initiator, who gives us the tests to overcome on our journey. Although it doesn't feel as if they are doing you a favour, that is exactly what is happening.

In my own soulmate encounter, for example, the person I was – or thought I was – disappeared! The 'victim' lurking deep in my shadow was pulled on to the stage and given a good shaking. I had never seen myself as a victim, but there she was, with no voice, no opinions and no rights to anything. I needed to accept my weak vulnerability and to discover that always being fine and strong was denying a side of me that I had learned early in my life was not appropriate to express. We don't have victims in my family – they just get on with things – the classic stiff upper lip is what earned you the strokes you wanted.

Another way to describe a dark night experience might be a spiritual emergence even though it feels more like an emergency. This can happen to those whose soul has decided it's time to wake up, and they find themselves drawn to explore healing, meditation, astrology or some other of the myriad metaphysical strands. At some point if feels as if you don't fit in any more with your friends or family. Your new spiritual experiences and under-standing seem to have put up a wall between you and the life you have lived for so many years. It feels as if you are tuned to a different radio station and it becomes increas-ingly difficult to be at ease with those who were (and possibly will be again) close to you. The visionary trans-personal psychotherapist Barbara Somers used to liken this situation to a blob of frogspawn from which we, as one egg, have become detached, no longer being part of the 'blob'. This brings a strong sense of isolation and loneli-ness as we are unable to go back, and yet not sure where the future lies. Eventually this one 'egg' meets up with others who are no longer part of their respective 'blobs' and a new community is formed, but without the constraints of tribal and cultural mythology that created a limiting container.

The soulmates involved here may be close friends or

family members. They will be the ones, initially, who make you feel as if you are weird because you've suddenly become impassioned about angels, Reiki, crystals or living in a yurt. They are putting fences in your path to see if you carry the conviction to jump them. They are pulling out of your shadow the feeling that you must conform or you will be ostracised. It is a difficult test which is asking you to put your soul in the driving seat of your life. The soulmate(s) who present the greatest challenge may actually feel threatened by the change that is taking place in you, and feel they are 'losing' you.

The soul has lifted you out of your old structure and the new one has not yet formed. At this stage it seems that all those meditations that gave you such uplift have lost their ability to do so. You feel totally alone and would do anything to get back on track. It seems as though you have become so sensitive that the grief and suffering of the entire planet rests on your own personal shoulders. As you 'shut down' on the world, there is a tremendous need to spend more time by yourself which further increases your sense of alienation.

This is all about breaking down the authority and autonomy of the ego, or little self. The ego is essentially an inflated bag of nothing, and although required in childhood to get us out into the world and give us some sense of identity, it is now time for it to relinquish its role of regent in deference to the arrival of the true monarch, the self or soul. It is not an easy abdication. For the personality suddenly to place its trust in a part of your nature that has not had much to do with the running of your life (apparently) until now feels like jumping off a cliff. A soulmate can give you the necessary push.

> Come to the edge.
> We might fall.
> Come to the edge.
> It's too high!
> COME TO THE EDGE!
> And they came
> and he pushed
> and they flew . . .
> CHRISTOPHER LOGUE ON *Apollinaire*

It seems as if all the mantras, meditations, affirmations, pleas, prayers and furniture arrangement that worked before now seem to hit a brick wall. Perhaps there's no one there after all and you've just changed one empty reality for another, even more 'unreal'. The books that seemed so full of truths feel dry and dusty. Peace? Love? Light? Nowhere to be found. Perhaps this therapist, that workshop, the clairvoyant, astrologer or tarot reader who solved your problems before will be able to help; *someone* will help with this turmoil and pain. But nothing seems to work. Functioning on auto-pilot and with nowhere to turn, now you are really on the floor. And invariably there'll be soulmates, particularly family ones, telling you to 'pull yourself together' and 'forget all that nonsense – look where it's got you!' The closer they are to you, the more influence they have in testing (and therefore deepening) your spiritual convictions.

The key words here are *surrender* and *trust* and they should be written in large illuminated script. This is the moment the soul has been waiting for. The resignation of the ego from its seat of power is not an easy experience, since it often feels as if it has been glued in place. But in this moment it has gone, and although it might stage a comeback at a later date, things will never be the same.

At some point a strange sense of peace and inner 'knowing' begins to pervade your being. This peace, which 'passeth all understanding', and this 'knowing' are *direct* experiences; they cannot be acquired, even if you read every book in the world. The dark night experience strips us naked, empties us out of anything false, reduces us to nothing, takes away our masks and scours our pot ready to be filled with clear fresh water. New wine needs new bottles, and our old bottles are very much older than we can imagine.

It is the process of transformation that is the difficult part.

> *What must the caterpillar do*
> *That it may one day fly?*

The caterpillar doesn't sprout wings – it actually *liquefies*. It has a very dark night of the soul in its chrysalis, caterpillar-style, and *totally* loses its old identity.

The greater the autonomy of the ego, the darker this experience needs to be. Our egos have built up walls and barriers, created masks and behaviour patterns throughout our lives, burying our true nature under these defences. From childhood onwards our egos are in control and mostly making sure that we become someone who we truly are not. Acceptable to society, yes, but not living according to our true blueprint. Egos cannot create that wholeness of the heart, which will end suffering, and in a sense the ego – in a dark night – realises that *it* is the problem. It stands between us and our deepest yearnings, always whispering that it knows the best way forward. In the darkest hour before the dawn, the ego surrenders to a power higher than itself, one that aligns us with our divinity and puts us back together again in a different way. Poor old ego, it thinks it has done a really good job through all these years and, in a sense, it has. But it is also a manipulative control freak with devious ways and subtle methods of achieving its own ends, and now needs to be relegated to middle management status. Now it is time to dance to a different drum, to change key and sing to a different tune.

Some of our old attributes and qualities of course will remain, but the realms of higher consciousness are unavailable to the ego. There have been, and are, many who walk the spiritual road whose egos become even more inflated. 'Now I am a *spiritual* master!' they announce. But at some point the lack of humility that goes with a pumped-up ego is spotted, and they come tumbling down from their plastic pedestals into the handful of devotees whose eyes have yet to be opened. Not much point in being a 'spiritual master' if you don't behave like one. As the old nursery rhyme goes:

> *A man of words and not of deeds*
> *Is like a garden full of weeds.*

So, in summary, a dark night of the soul is not a *prerequisite* to the opening of your spiritual nature, but it is mentioned here because such an experience may be triggered by a soulmate – a dark knight or lady of the soul. At some point further down the road, you will be able to see what a powerful punctuation mark in your life your meeting with them has been.

Perhaps someone you dearly loved died, as happened to Sarah. An attractive woman in her sixties, her beloved son and soulmate, Martin, had died from an asthma attack three years before she came for a past life regression. Her grief had taken her life from her and she couldn't seem to pull herself together. She had had many incarnations with this soul, now her son in this lifetime. They had been lovers, siblings and parents to each other and the soul-mate bond was deep and powerful. His loss in this life-time precipitated a very dark night for her soul. It pulled the grief of loss and separation that had repeated through many lifetimes, when one or other of them had died, out of her shadow, offering her a choice. Would she now see that although she couldn't actually touch him, he was always only a thought away? The body had gone, but the love was eternal, and this was a real test of her beliefs.

The loss of someone you love and adore, whether by death or desertion, can cause free-fall into despair. There seems to be no point in carrying on, the lights have gone out and the heart is so heavy it feels like a boulder in the chest, but the importance of understanding how our shadows influence our lives cannot be underestimated. It could be said that there's already so much darkness about the place that we don't need any more to fuel the fires of fear. The point here being that the darkness 'out there' is created by our own suppressed collective shadows. Our inner terrorists, despots, suicide bombers and control freaks are insisting on being owned. We also have inner saints, magicians, kings, queens and angels whose potential has also been suppressed. How dare we think so small?

But it is gold that lies hidden in the shadow, full of unrealised feelings and potential. If we can just have the courage to peer into its dark well we will be given a powerful opportunity to rebuild our world in a different way and finally to let go of the family and tribal mythology that may have bent us so out of shape that we finally broke up into pieces.

Projections: the Me in You

It may feel as if this whole business of soulmates is more like a bed of nails than roses. The relevance of understanding our shadows in the context of soulmates is because the qualities we have hidden in our shadow bag, when denied and disowned, will often be projected on to others 'out there'. Understanding the dynamic of projection is vitally important, and crucial to becoming aware of what lies hidden in our own shadows. None of us knows ourselves. If you asked someone to describe the sort of person they were, even the most honest and self-investigative of us would give a description of themselves that is hardly recognisable from how that person might be described by their husband, wife or lover. Ask that person's children, or workmate what they think and other portraits appear. We will always see ourselves through tinted lens. As Liz Greene, astrologer and Jungian psychologist states:

> *We are usually not aware of our deepest motivations, and, given this degree of blindness, are hardly in a position to be aware of anybody else's.*

A projection, therefore, is a hidden quality, trait or characteristic of our own that we react to when experienced in another. It's like throwing a brick at a cinema screen when we have a strong reaction to something we see on it. We need to have a look at the film in the projector as being the source of the image. When a person projects an unconscious quality existing within themselves on to another person, they react as if that quality belongs to the other. The reaction will often be irrational and highly charged. Projections, which can take a lifetime to introject, or own for ourselves, can be both positive and negative, and it takes only a simple test to discover what shadow figures we have repressed or refused to claim.

At this point it is worth stopping for a moment to draw up a list of the main qualities you might be looking for in a loving soulmate relationship, and those you don't want. Limit it to four on each side:

Qualities I Look For	*Qualities I Don't Want*
Humour	Rigidity
Tolerance	Workaholism
Sensitivity	Timebound
Adventurousness	Volatility

Could you consider whether those qualities, on both sides, might also belong to you? As well as the qualities you have listed, now go through the same exercise with people. On one side the ones you admire, respect and think the world of, and on the other the ones who you despise, drive you mad or definitely dislike (and why).

People I like or Admire	*People I don't Like*
My next-door neighbour (calm and strong)	G.W. Bush (he's a bully)

Soulmates

My cousin, Sarah	John at work
(always cheerful)	(he's self-obsessed)
Billy Connolly	Uncle Joe
(sensitive and very funny)	(don't trust him)
Oprah Winfrey	BBC newscaster (she looks
(she's making a difference)	so pleased with herself)

Projections are not just limited to individuals. Organisations, religions, ideologies, skin colours and creeds may be the target. The hallmark of a projection is not so much the viewpoint as the intensity and charge of the reaction.

> *Everything that is unconscious in ourselves, we discover in Our neighbour, and treat him accordingly.*
> C.G. JUNG, *Memories, Dreams and Reflections*

Is a homophobe covering up a latent potential in themselves? Is a vehement capitalist, communist or fundamentalist of any kind shouting so loudly in order not to hear the whisper of their own inner opposite? Road rage is a contemporary example of projection. A total inability to accept and deal with some inner frustration drives people to commit violence against another for some petty motoring offence.

When we feel an overwhelming dislike towards someone, we are in touch with a long-buried, unacceptable trait in ourselves. When rage, envy, shame, blame or greed uncontrollably flood our senses, it is an overflow from the shadow. But in this shadow, if we dare to shine a light in there, we will find 'pure gold' as Jung stated. And in relationships is where the shadow will find a stage to express itself. If we can face the inner demons that our soulmates drag out of our shadow bags, bringing them into the drama of our everyday life, it stops them from leaping out of the wings and overwhelming us. It is our soulmates who hold the mirror so close to our face that we may not be able to bear it. But the soul is insisting that we own our shadow and will draw towards it more of the same until we become aware of and own what is really ours.

Jekyll or Hide?

Each of us is like Dr Jekyll, denying the existence of the dark and distorted Mr Hyde. This extraordinary tale, immortalised by Robert Louis Stevenson who wrote it in 1886, has a similarity to Mary Shelley's *Frankenstein*, written nearly seventy years earlier. Both are parables about the shadow side of our selves, and involve scientists who find the constraints of society so unbearable that they create an alter ego to live out their 'unacceptable passions'. Significantly, the first victim of both of these creations is a child. The story of Jekyll and Hyde (being a pun on 'hide' or hidden) opens with two men passing a mysterious cellar door in a basement (representing the subconscious mind) where the sinister, deformed Mr Hyde apparently lives. They later discover that this door is connected in an L-shaped way to the home of Dr Jekyll. By taking a potion he has concocted, Jekyll is able to transform into Hyde and carry out his acts of depravity without guilt or remorse. He believes that the soul is made up of good and evil, and it is his quest to find a substance that, when ingested, will separate the two so that they do not have to live in bondage to each other and in constant competition. Of course, as the story reveals, it is not so simple and Mr Hyde (the shadow) begins to take over and ultimately kills himself, thus releasing both of them. The message is, as with the tale of Frankenstein, that we are not *either* our shadow self *or* the persona we present to the world, but *both*, and if we can muster the courage at least to recognise the parts of our selves that are hidden then we are well on our way to becoming a whole and balanced person.

The more active Mr Hyde (our shadow) becomes, the more Dr Jekyll (the face we present to the world) over-compensates and denies his existence by becoming more 'religious' in his attempt to distance himself and in order not to be overwhelmed by his dark-natured Mr Hyde. Perhaps here we have a clue to paedophile priests, violent religious fundamentalists and the likes of Dr Shipman, the serial killer. History is littered with figures who show us the dark potential of the extreme negative side of our nature from Genghis Khan, Nero, Hitler, Pol Pot, Slobodan Milosevic, Fred and Rosemary West, Ian Brady and Myra Hindley to contemporary world leaders such as Robert Mugabe and Saddam Hussein. On the other hand there are figures as light as those mentioned are dark. We only have to think of the Dalai Lama and we can feel warmed by his humour and gentleness even after he's experienced, as Nelson Mandela, extreme suffering at the hands of others. We have all got a murderer as well as a saint latent within. We are both Jekyll and Hyde.

Since we are now in the time of releasing our past karmic residues and sorting out our unfinished soul business that has been accumulating over the centuries, we can begin to see that our souls are trying to clear the slate for a fresh start. This means that all the hubris of the shadow will be regurgitated or, as decreed by the Kali Yuga, history will repeat itself, not only collectively, but individually. We are being emotionally sick at the moment, clearing our systems. If we daren't deal with it personally, then we will do it vicariously through the soaps on TV – no longer 'everyday stories of country folk', but violent displays of extreme human emotion – or the media and global events. We have created our sick world by repressing our collective and 'unacceptable' traits that now terrorise us.

> *He who calls forth that which is within him,*
> *That which is within him, shall save him.*
> *He who does not call forth that which is within him,*
> *That which is within him shall destroy him.*
> JESUS, FROM THE GOSPEL OF THE ESSENES

Or, as Plato said, 'The life which is unexamined is not worth living.' Perhaps it is worth reconsidering here, as we did in Chapter 3, the difference between the energy of the *emotions* and those that are *feelings* from the soul, because our soulmates will play an integral part in our awareness of and differentiation between these two energies. We will now have a look at how we attract soulmates into our lives and what form they may take.

are you my soulmate?

Give me a Clue

You have been mine before –
How long ago I may not know:
But just when at that swallow's soar
Your neck turned so,
Some veil did fall – I knew it all of yore.

DANTE GABRIEL ROSSETTI

This quote by Rossetti speaks of a certain type of recognition between soulmates, but we have learned that soulmates are certainly not exclusively of this variety. Recognising that someone is a soulmate is not difficult, since it depends on the degree of energy that exists between you and the other. Wherever and with whomever you have a powerful feeling, the soulmate dynamic is at work. Soulmate recognition is not always an instantaneous affair. It may dawn on you gradually, until you suddenly realise you have got them 'under your skin'. This slow dawning may feel like two dancers circling each other before coming together for the next part of the dance, or it may be more like two stags, sizing one another up before locking horns.

The question of whether or not a certain person is a soulmate of yours should by now have become superfluous in the light of the information contained in the previous chapters. The more important question to ask yourself is what is this person for whom you have these feelings doing in your life? Your body is the best litmus test for soulmate connections. If someone is having an impact on you, your body may respond in the lower part of your abdomen – the sacral chakra – fuelling the sexual fire which will draw you together for the next episode. It may affect your solar plexus, giving you feelings of 'butterflies' in your stomach – or knotted guts – whenever you think about them, or are in their presence. You may feel it in your heart chakra as a physical 'heartache', yearning or pain or as if your heart is going to burst. Or your throat may be affected, making you feel speechless and constricted in the chakra of communication, or alternatively suddenly finding that words are coming out of your mouth like water from a fountain. This is the body and soul working together, tapping you on the shoulder to look more deeply into 'what's going on'.

The Tuning Fork Effect

The force that will draw you to another is similar to what goes on with a tuning fork. A tuning fork is used, among other things, to adjust sounds in musical instruments. A human tuning fork has the same effect on us. When we 'hear' a sound in another, our being sets up a resonant response. Somewhere within us we recognise this note. It 'strikes a chord' with us and is about tuning in to the sound of our soul. Once this sound has been responded to, it is as if a wavelength is set up between ourselves and the person with whom we feel this effect. We even use this terminology – being 'in tune' or 'on the same wavelength' – to describe our relationships with soulmates. Not so strange, really, when you consider that the emperor moth can locate a specific mate from a distance of eight miles simply by picking up the vibes of their pheromones on the ether. How much more likely that we can do the same.

This tuning fork effect will be the one at work when you walk into a room full of people and are immediately 'drawn' to one person. This is because their soul note has a resonant frequency with your own. When you begin to get to know this person that you 'already know', you may notice that there are certain mannerisms or quirks that seem familiar. There is a sense that even their physical features are familiar. In fact 'familiar' is the word that applies to everything about them. This doesn't mean that we take on bodies that look like the ones we have inhabited before; it is the internal tuning fork of resonance at work. All of us have brought forward into this lifetime information that will be seeking attention and will 'recognise' its counterpart. Perhaps it is something about the shape of their feet, or the curve of their neck that you seem to recognise. For some people, the shape of hands is important; perhaps they had a deep love for someone whose hands were formed in a certain way and the sight of similar hands triggers that sense of familiarity, even though the story or drama that was played out together in the past remains sealed in the unconscious memory banks. Colour of hair and eyes, shapes of faces and stature may also give clues to past encounters with soulmates which you are drawn to re-enact in the here and now.

The tuning fork effect also works conversely, and can

produce an 'instant dislike'. Here, the note emanating from the other person is familiar, it has a resonance with you, but repulses you rather than magnetises. This reaction needs just as much attention as the more appealing tuning fork effect because, again, it's telling you that there is unfinished business between you and that person that still carries a charge.

Where are we most likely to find our soulmates?

Marriage and Committed Partnerships

These are probably the most obvious place to look for a soulmate in all their different permutations. This is the place where our expectations and projections concerning the happily ever after myth will be most active.

There are many who will tell of meeting someone for the first time and feeling as if they had known them for ever – which they probably have. But what if you are already in a committed relationship? Like Christine and Simon. Christine was already married with two children when she met Simon, single and several years younger. They knew, from the depths of their souls, that they had to be together. Past life work revealed that they had been lovers and were to be married, but the Second World War loomed. He was killed in France, and she suffered inconsolable and permanent grief. Did they *look* the same in this incarnation? No, but the feel, the tuning fork resonance was there and unmistakable. Time will reveal what soul work will be addressed through their twenty-first-century reunion.

What about the deserted husband? He now has to deal with the issues of grief and loss that have been brought into focus by Christine and his daughters' departure. This seems to be a typical contemporary (and age-old) scenario. A man and woman fall in love, perhaps they reflect back to the other their ideals in a 'perfect' partnership. They value and respect one another, and the mutual sense of commitment they both bring to the relationship. Then one day one or other of them is swept off their feet by a 'soulmate'. Suddenly life is exciting and meaningful. Which of these two is really a soulmate?

In truth both of them are. This is a karmic stitch-up for which there is no straightforward answer. There is a complex and potent mix of issues involved in such a triangular situation – betrayer/betrayed, guilt/righteousness, stability/change, commitment/intransigence – and it is almost as if a potion has been taken by the two lovers who feel they must spend the rest of their lives together. This must be one of the hardest decisions to make in romantic soulmate situations. Leaving your marriage partner, who may be a very kind and loving person, will bring all sorts of issues of the soul to the surface. Shall I go, or should I stay? Needless to say there is not a simple answer to this. We often hear, 'I can't possibly leave him, how would he cope without me?' But perhaps his soul needs the opportunity to find out, to see if the love or affection he had for you could go the whole nine yards, freeing you to go to find happiness elsewhere, and moving beyond ownership. Hopefully the one who is left can be mature enough to be able, perhaps further down the line, to sustain friendship. These things happen to challenge us, to see what emerges and to take us beyond re-actionary responses.

Then there are the soulmates who stay together, even

though they can't stand one another. Whatever it was that brought them together has long since vanished over the horizon. Their days are spent sending barbed comments, criticising and running each other down, or perpetuating a personal cold war. This is a toxic environment for the soul and while it may be economically impossible for them to live apart, these soulmates are asking each other to put down their weapons and call a heartfelt truce. Every partnership, as far as the soul is concerned, is about growth and understanding who we, as individuals, are.

> *We are the mirror as well as the face in it.*
> *We are tasting the taste this minute of eternity.*
> *We are pain and what cures pain.*
> *We are the sweet cold water and the jar that pours.*
> JALALUDDIN RUMI

The mirror of reflection, in the initial 'in love' stage, offers a revelation of sparkling joy. Everybody loves a lover because they actually seem to radiate. Then, mostly the face in the mirror starts to alter and we begin to notice there are some blemishes we seemed to have overlooked in the beginning. If the heart is involved, then the odd wart here and there will make no difference; on the contrary, they become endearing. If the reverse is true, then before too long *everything* seems to become a trial and an irritation and the situation moves from having them 'under your skin' to 'up your nose'.

'Even the way she squeezes the toothpaste tube drives me mad!'

'I can't stand the way he leaves his tea bags in the sink!'

'He just comes in and slumps in front of the box.'

'She never kisses me when I come home, like she used to.'

What's happened? The magic has worn off, and what remains? When did passion and joy wither like an unwatered flower? Is this old slipper really my soulmate? Perhaps part of the problem is that we have put our faith and trust in institutions and marriage is one of them. But we can become 'institutionalised' and love and passion fly out of the window, leaving us to live in a colourless, but possibly comfortable, rut. We often hear, 'They lived together for years, and as soon as they got married, it all seemed to go wrong.' The one who seemed to be a soulmate has become an ordinary person, with irritating habits and interests that are in conflict with your own. Now the work begins as the real purpose of this soulmate connection emerges when the rose-coloured spectacles fall to the floor. Marriage in this case has changed the dynamic of the relationship. A 'wife' is somehow different from a 'partner' or 'lover'. Structure often seems to clip the wings of love; commitment without freedom can feel like being boxed in, and the soul feels constraint. While it may seem that family values are the casualties of this change, perhaps it is part of a process that will lead us to expand our concept of 'family'. Sitting down together and speaking from the heart can begin to shift the dynamic of your relationship to its next stage. As the Arabic saying goes: 'What comes from the heart is heard by the heart.'

The Family

Another common soulmate meeting ground is the family arena, where soul themes will be kick-started by one or both parents and then the thread picked up in later life by another soulmate, just in case the issue has escaped our attention. Our early life sets the scene for our soulmate encounters further down the line. The little girl whose father left home believes that somehow it was her fault. As an adult she may meet men who always leave. Her soulmate father (in agreement with her at a soul level) set her up to look more deeply into why she feels unworthy of a man's love. It's not the truth. When she has done some work on herself, can value and love herself, then she has cleared the abandonment issue and her relationships will change. The tuning fork will have changed its pitch.

A mother from hell in a family has agreed to play the soulmate 'fall guy' for the sake of giving her children's souls the challenge of finding their own individuality. Some parents feel that their children must be 'chips off the old block', which is like insisting that an apple should be an orange. There may be an angry, alcoholic or depressed parent (soulmate) in the family. A child will feel threatened and unsafe when such a person is around, as their actuely sensitive receptors pick up the vibes in these situations, but they provide the ground for soulwork later in life. They will encounter the same qualities that scared or intimidated them in childhood, in their partners, bosses or 'friends'.

Soulmates at Work

Our soulmate encounters may be through our work environment, another place where close contact with others is unavoidable. What is your bullying employer really trying to tell you? Who is there at work with whom you feel tension or anxiety? Does this feeling they engender in you make working creatively difficult? Perhaps there is someone in a position of authority who evokes those feelings you can remember having as a child when you felt as if you had no right to express your opinions and somehow they weren't valid anyway. It is no accident that you have a colleague who makes you bristle, or a chairman whom you despise.

No Escape?

No meeting of any significance is an accident. In fact there are no such things as accidents. It was no 'accident' that you happened to drop your book just at that moment and it was picked up by someone whose eyes held you in their gaze. It was no accident that you decided 'on the spur of the moment' to go to the party where you met the one who is now woven into the fabric of your being.

Don't we have a choice, then, about the people we meet? Not really. We have a choice as to whether we get involved with them or not, but if there is unresolved karmic business between the two of you, it is unlikely that you will be able to walk away. This is soul business, and beyond the abilities of the personality to interfere at this stage. When it is *time* to meet with that important person, your paths will cross, no matter what. How could we possibly resist the power of our internal tuning forks and factory-installed chakra microchips directing us into situations where interaction with another is a call from the soul?

> But we, like sentries, are obliged to stand
> In starless nights and wait the 'pointed hour
> JOHN DRYDEN

Since soulmates are not necessarily those with whom we will walk off into the sunset to live happily ever after, what sort of people are they?

Different Sorts of Soulmate: the Good, the Bad and the Ugly

It might seem that our soul and its group sit up there in conference and then send various members down to earth to be knocked into shape; something like detailing a platoon of men to go off into a war zone. But even in the most difficult of life contracts that we sign up for there will be a soulmate somewhere in the background who is not a sergeant major, but one who reminds us that we are okay, and love does exist, even though at times it feels as if we have landed on an alien planet. When I talk about love, I don't mean romantic love, I mean the heartfelt love that comes without conditions and strings attached. This can be felt in the presence of:

Soul Companions

These are souls who have been comrades, friends, brothers-at-arms or women friends through many lifetimes. Your relationship with them may include, but will not be complicated by sexual attraction and their trust and love goes deep and is without judgement. You know and accept each other for who you are and there is a certain feeling of peace which comes from just knowing that this companion is on the planet, even if geographical distance may come between you. The thread of friendship is always picked up when you meet, as if life has made no difference to your steadfast affection even though it has taken you in opposite directions. We may end up living with or even marrying a soul companion, since it is someone we feel comfortable with, who doesn't push our buttons and provides a stable home base, perhaps for the soul to deal with other issues. It also happens that we get lives of respite from intense soul drama. Time on earth lived in peace and quiet gives us the chance to appreciate the wonder of it.

Mentor Soulmates

If, or when, a soul incarnates into a difficult family situation, the world can seem a fearful and frightening place. It's not easy for the soul to stay present in family situations where there is violence, alcoholism, fear or a lack of warmth and love. Sometimes there will be 'imaginary friends' around a child who sees and communicates with them, although no one else can. These will be soulmates from their soul group, helping the soul to adjust to living on earth and providing reassurance that there's someone around to help them make sense of it all. Unfortunately, if a child speaks about their 'friends' that no one else can see they may be told not to be so silly, or 'It's just your imagination.' This can create a conflict in the child's mind about what is 'real' and result in their intuitive (third eye) faculty becoming judged as an unreliable way of seeing things.

But there are other kinds of mentor soulmates who often appear for a child experiencing a difficult and loveless childhood. They come in the physical shape of grannies, grandpas, a kindly uncle, aunt or even neighbour, who provide the child's soul with love, encouragement and a sense of being 'seen' as it struggles to make sense of life on earth.

If there is no one with two legs, there may be one with four. One of my own vivid past life memories was as a small boy born to emotionally remote Victorian parents. But there was a dog in the family who shared my secrets and adventures, and gave my life meaning and a sense of being connected to some living creature. Unfortunately one day my wonderful four-legged friend had gone. I couldn't find him anywhere. I can't remember what my parents told me had happened to him, all I knew was that I now felt totally alone. The sense of loss followed me through the rest of that lifetime. Animals, with their unconditional love and loyalty, provide many people with the companionship they seem unable to find through human contact and are a source of comfort to elderly people who are on their own. They might not exactly fit the consensus view of a soulmate, but they certainly fulfil a vital role.

The Brillo Pad

This category of soulmate is what this book is mostly about. The abrasive (and even abusive) behaviour directed towards us by these soulmates is really a heavily disguised blessing which offers as great an opportunity for growth as the degree of discomfort we experience from their presence in our lives. There will be a button-pushing Brillo Pad in everyone's life. They are most likely to be found in the situations mentioned before, of family, partnership and work. Or you might find a Brillo Pad living next door. 'Don't tell me my nightmare neighbour is a soulmate!'

Why not? They are certainly pressing your buttons about something. Why can't you stand them? Too noisy, chaotic, disapproving – disrupting your ordered lifestyle? How you deal with your feelings and them is the all-important lesson.

Family Brillo Pads also bring up a lot of 'stuff' for us. The mother-in-law who feels threatened by someone taking her son's attention and uses emotional blackmail to get her own way, siblings with their painful pecking orders, children who are here to polish off their parents. Brillo Pads at work can also become obsessions until we fathom out what they are making us face. Simpering and subservient or frighteningly authoritative, scapegoating and victimising – these soulmates echo previous past life situations where our interaction with them left a *samskara* that needs releasing now. Then there are extreme Brillo Pads . . .

Violent Soulmates

These would seem like a contradiction in terms, according to the old view of what a soulmate might be. This seemingly unpleasant variety of soulmate will be encountered, again, in the family or relationship department, although there are those who suffer isolated incidents of violence in their lives. It is often the one most fearful of such an event to whom it happens, demonstrating the tuning fork and electro-magnetic principles of the law of attraction at work. What about violent partnerships? Increasing cases of domestic violence are being reported where the woman is battered about by her partner, but then goes back for more. What's happening here? Is *this* a soulmate connection?

Most definitely. This is a situation when the polarities of bully/victim or master/slave are being acted out. A bully needs a victim and a victim needs someone to reinforce their lack of power. The soul is asking the bully why there is a need to hit and punch someone who is helpless, and the victim needs to get into their own power, to stand their ground and say, 'This is unacceptable, I'm leaving!' But bullies can also be beguiling. 'I'm so sorry. I really love you. I won't do it again.' The element of fear involved in this situation cauterises communication. Violence begets more violence or creates a paralysis in the victim that makes it impossible to leave. The fear of staying is almost easier to cope with than the fear of them coming after you, with dire consequences. This situation requires outside help, or round the circuit of co-dependency it will go again. But as the Talmud says:

> *Be wary of making a woman cry*
> *God counts all her tears*

Sexual Soulmates

These are the ones who were drawn, and stay, together because of the powerful chemistry of sex. Most people's ideas about soulmates include the union of bodies as well as souls. Our souls were called into existence through the sexual union of our parents and all of us have experienced our sexuality in one way or another. Sex is a *natural* thing to do. It is a biological imperative not just to guarantee survival of the species, but to experience the oneness we have forgotten: the joy of being with the body and yet to be free of it. Sex that is centred solely on the lower chakras is not a 'whole' experience, and has certainly become 'unholy'. The repression of our sexual natures over the past 200 years or so has now erupted into the opposite polarity, of sex everywhere. It sells cars and coffee, is on our TV screens, billboards and in magazines – sex is out of its closet.

Physical attraction can play a large part in soulmate relationships where there is work to be done. The possibility for soul union is held within each sexual encounter, but it does not depend on positions, breathing techniques, holding of sexual energies or particular practices according to a handbook. When the heart and mind are also included, something altogether different takes place. Sexual soulmates are asking each other to include these other ingredients in their union. In the meantime, because the sexual chemistry is so strong – even addictive – the connection to this partner remains intense.

The Feather Duster

This variety of soulmate might also be called a Warm Blanket. These soulmates are different from the companion or mentor variety in that their appearance in your life will not necessarily be a permanent fixture. They seem to appear out of nowhere just when you need them. Perhaps they help you put the pieces of your life together again after some shattering experience. Perhaps they soothe your troubled brow, hold your hand through a difficult situation, or help you walk again when you've been knocked to the floor. The effect of emotional trauma needs a soulmate to help us re-establish our connection to life. These healing soulmates don't tell you what to do, unless they're asked. They won't tell you to pull yourself together or that you'll get over it – they are simply there for the time that you need them. Not for long, perhaps, but returning a favour you bestowed on them in a previous life. What goes around always comes around.

Cross-Cultural Soulmates

These are the ones you might 'bump' into if work or a holiday takes you to another part of the world. Our souls do not confine their earthly experiences to one culture, gender or colour of skin. Meeting a soulmate who has incarnated into a different ethnic background from your own can raise a host of issues, if you should go beyond friendship into marriage. Crossing cultural divides is an enormous challenge and may be more than the relationship can tolerate if one or other is unable to step into the middle ground. What is the western man searching for in an oriental woman? Or the Shirley Valentine looking for in a passionate Latin lover? If you have always been drawn to men of African origin, or dark-eyed Spanish women, your inner tuning fork, or the energy of a *samskara*, is sounding to the familiarity of those cultures because there's work to be done. These soulmates are asking us to move beyond the divisions and boundaries that we have created between colours, creeds, cultures, races or ages. Behind these masks we are all souls in various stages of evolution and awareness. No one is better than another – just different.

So is it a case of opposites attract, or like attracts like, with soulmates? Both of these forces may apply. We have seen, from looking at our shadow nature, how we project the unacknowledged and hidden sides of ourselves on to others and then react when confronted by them. So we may be attracted to a soulmate who is similar to us, or who shows us an opposite. Two extroverts together might produce the same nightmare as a pair of introverts trying to make a go of their relationship. The law of attraction is not hard and fast. Opposites, similarities, either or both may appear in the mirror of reflection as we look to find the hidden faces of our selves in others. It is soulmates in all their different shapes and sizes who help us to look at and remove the specks on the soul that keep us from expanding into love without limitation.

The purpose of a soulmate may not be clear until your relationship with them is over. Endings can precipitate a nosedive into bitterness, anger, jealousy, guilt, remorse, and genuine sadness that it hasn't worked out as you had imagined. All of these are the energies of the *samskaras* that stand between us and the realisation that love is actually the glue that holds everything together.

Because of the times we are in, the push from the soul to move us beyond the storms of the lower three chakras becomes more urgent. 'Move to the mountain-top of the heart,' it cries. 'No!' says the personality. 'This pain, this rage, is where I am, where I belong.' In the wider scheme of things, does it *really* matter that she left, cleaned you out financially, went to bed with your best friend? You are still alive, and although it seems as if there has been a total eclipse of the sun, who knows what this situation has freed you to do with your life? Surely not to spend the rest of it like a broken reed. It's only life. It's a drama of the soul and ultimately you will put down your script and go backstage, where you will meet all the others involved in this particular play, and swap notes about it all.

An inability to get beyond feelings of guilt or betrayal simply means that we will have to repeat the performance over and over again until we finally arrive at the place where we can say, 'Ouch! This really hurts but I prefer to turn the pain into something useful. This has happened to give me the chance to overcome it.'

> *Your pain is the breaking of the shell that encloses your*
> *understanding.*
> *Even as the stone of the fruit must break, that its heart may*
> *stand*
> *in the sun, so must you know pain.*
> KAHLIL GIBRAN, *The Prophet*

This is the story of Amena, which demonstrates how soulmates set the scene for her in this lifetime (her parents), another soulmate reinforced her focus on the area needing attention (her husband), a further soulmate entered her life to help her redeem herself – and then left. Amena is a beautiful, blue-eyed blonde, who was born to parents who needed parenting themselves. They lived in Kenya, when the age of colonialism still retained its influence over those who had remained there after it had gained its independence. Caught in a time-warp where the old rules about children still applied, she and her elder brother Richard were supposed to be 'seen but not heard' and were certainly not supposed to interfere with their parents' pursuit of pleasure, especially her mother, who was an integral part of what was known as the 'Happy Valley' set.

The two little children were packed off to boarding school at the tender ages of five and seven, by which time Amena had discovered that she could get care and attention by making herself ill, and her body soon cottoned on to this method of being nurtured by producing boils all over itself when she was four. She would put stones into her nostrils and ears, telling herself that she could 'catch a bug' by doing this, and get the attention her little soul was craving.

Eventually her parents separated, although their marriage had been only a label, and her father remarried, giving the children – teenagers by now – some sense of family life without the presence of her beautiful, attention-seeking, alcoholic mother. Returning to England, Amena launched herself on a successful career as a film producer, making commercials for several well-known companies, as her personal life careened out of control with the use of drink and drugs. After several affairs, she married another 'victim of life' – Julian – and they produced a son. Her increasing fear of the world was blanketed by her increasing use of alcohol. Her husband, also successful in the 'real' world as a film director, was becoming increasingly dependent on whisky to get him through his day.

Finally this vortex spun out of control when Amena met and found love in the arms of another woman. The needy child had finally found someone to look after her, and this was the turning point. This woman, Rachel, after a particularly alcoholic episode, steered Amena towards the ladder that would help her climb out of the well she had been floundering in. No sooner had she begun to emerge from the clutches of vodka than she was diagnosed as having a cancerous tumour in her right lung, demonstrating that our bodies are always involved with what is happening in our minds and to our feelings. Bodies take a little longer, being denser, to demonstrate their dis-ease at the state we are in, and lungs are directly connected to the heart (have I the heart to continue?) chakra, and the throat (can I trust my self to speak my own truth?).

'I wouldn't have survived without Rachel,' Amena says now. 'I just couldn't have coped.' And then what happened? Her lover and carer for ten years fell in love with another woman. This could have meant a return to the well of despair for Amena, but because of the support and self-examination process that she had undergone through her meetings with AA, she had the spiritual good sense to know how and the strength and will to cope with this next of her hurdles. She realised that without Rachel she might never have got her life together and become her own person, as she is today. Of course it was the most painful of separations, but she also realised that her relationship with Rachel would always be intact – they are soulmates after all – just as Rachel and her new lover had and still have their own relationship.

This is a major leap in understanding. We do not and cannot 'own' anyone else. People are not like possessions, and while we may not physically be in their company, the continuum of love still exists between two people, unless it becomes contaminated with the energies of betrayal, guilt and all the other ingredients that swirl about and are linked to past scripts from old dramas that we need to let go of. If Amena had allowed herself to focus on what she might have felt as yet another person 'letting her down', following in the footsteps of her parents, her boyfriends and her husband, she would still be struggling in the gerbil's wheel of co-dependency.

Soulmates

We have now turned the matter of soulmates upside down and inside out. We have looked at them from every angle: how they became soulmates, the effect they have on us and why, the unseen forces that are at work in any soulmate encounter, what they might look like and where to find them. The next chapter will help you find your balance if you have been or are being blown off course by a soulmate experience.

how to cope
Help! And Where to Find It

To a mind that is still
The whole universe surrenders
CHANG TZU

Whether your experience of a soulmate is diabolic or divine, by now the *value* of all relationships is becoming clearer. 'Know thyself' commanded the Delphic oracle, and it is only through relationships that we can come to know more about our selves. This getting to know yourself is not easy, what with all our past lives and their *samskaras* stacked up behind us, our chakras waiting to have their buttons pressed, an internal tuning fork, like a time bomb, waiting to twang when a soulmate hoves into view, not to mention what we have stuffed into our shadow bags that we don't really want to look at. All this may seem a daunting prospect for the spiritual soul-searching traveller. But take heart. Soulmates, as we know by now, are the most valuable assets our soul has to help us polish away the grime of the ages, allowing the lantern within each and every one of us to shine. Being polished to a shine involves bodies, minds and souls, and these three aspects of our being all require attention, so this chapter is concerned with how to cope, where to find help, heal any wounds and move on. It's all about balance, something we lose when one of the not-so-happily-ever-after soulmates becomes involved with our lives.

Contact with someone who helps rub the sleep from our eyes is something to be celebrated even if it does feel more like a poke in the ribs than a gentle nudge into awareness. As humans we like to stay in our comfort zones. We don't want to be shaken or stirred and will take the safe or easy option in order not to destabilise the status quo. Our souls, however, have other ideas about our destiny, since the end of an epoch heralds the opportunity for moving to another level of consciousness – or else repeating the whole cycle again. Like a chickpea, we require quite a bit of cooking. Since it's not just hearts and minds that have been involved in soulmate experiences, but also bodies and souls, we need to consider healing in its widest sense for all our different and diverse 'bodies'. The very first step on the road to understanding and recovery is to GET HELP.

Help for the Body

Although sometimes slow to respond, our bodies, being the densest aspect of ourselves, will most definitely feel the effects of a soulmate encounter. Eczema, psoriasis, digestive problems, sleeplessness, loss of hair and appetite (or bingeing), aches, pains, blood pressure increases or visual problems may be some of the signs of the body speaking its mind about the situation. You may find yourself free-falling into depression either during or after an intense soulmate interlude, reaching for the Prozac or brandy to muffle the feelings of pain, betrayal, loss, grief, abandonment or pointlessness.

But there are other ways of helping to stabilise yourself that don't just create more problems for your system. We're talking bodies here, and regular sessions with a good complementary practitioner will help you to move through (or manage) internal storms. These people are like gardeners for the body and soul. Orthodox medicine is good for mechanical failure, but a homeopath, acupuncturist or cranio-sacral therapist will attend to the needs of the *whole* of you. They don't plaster over the cracks with chemical antidotes, but will pay attention to your entire energy system, helping it to find the strength to restore equilibrium.

After I had 'escaped' from Egypt and my own soulmate, I found myself facing crises of a different nature. My body was telling me that it couldn't take another step in the 'right' direction by producing a pain in my right leg that made me think of imminent Zimmer frames. The centre of my chest broke out in inflamed and itching eczema (heart chakra) and my sleep pattern was completely up the creek as a result of surviving on catnaps for nearly three years. I also faced a crisis in my work. How dare I work as a therapist and teacher of spiritual understandings when I couldn't sort out my own life? Actually I could hardly function at any level.

But 'someone' was looking after me as I was directed to an acupuncturist whose needles seemed to puncture the taut bubble of bottled-up emotions that had invaded every cell and atom. I have never cried like that, from the very bottom of my well. Relief, regret, all the fear I had carried on a daily basis seemed to pour out of me through the pins he had put in my body. This was my first step towards healing. He also recommended t'ai chi to help my body restore its confidence in movement. A dear friend, trained in reflexology, would come and do my feet, leaving me to sleep when she had finished. I swallowed copious quantities of Rescue Remedy as I struggled to get back into my body, the body that had been such a frightening place to live in. Living with fear has a paralysing effect. It seems as if all the systems except for red alert simply shut down. I could only cope with simple things. Reading (my great love), writing, birdsong, friends, woods and rivers had all disappeared. I felt *empty* – and that was the most important part of it all. My terrifying and wonderful soulmate had cracked me right open, drained me of just about everything I knew of as my self. It was as if, for the first time, I could feel my soul gently entering my being.

An acupuncturist helped *me*, but some people can't cope with the thought of needles (tortured past life coming through!), and although it is a fast track to releasing some of the emotions that have become locked into your system, there are other ways. A homeopath can be of great support in getting to root causes in a totally non-invasive way. A cranio-sacral therapist will also gently encourage your body back to balance. Homeopathic remedies, along with the Bach flower essences, are available these days in mainstream chemist shops. There are also the powerful Australian Bush Flower Essences, all of which – because of their subtle nature – work on the auric field and the subtle anatomy. This kind of panacea for problems is called vibrational medicine and I recommend you read a copy of Dr Richard Gerber's book, *A Practical Guide to Vibrational Medicine,* or *The Flower Essence Repertory* by Patricia Kaminski and Richard Katz, both of which are comprehensive guides to what essences are appropriate for your feelings. You may, for instance, need to take a few drops of vine essence every day to help you let go of trying to control some situation, or walnut to support you through change. Aspen will help you stop shaking with fear and crab apple with guilt and self-hatred that can appear when you feel as if you have been rejected by a soulmate.

Your chakras, as part of your energy field, will also have been affected by your intense emotions, so notice which colours you are drawn to – and that includes colours of food. I was only able to eat beetroot, carrots and oranges in my darkest days, which was telling me that my root and sacral chakras were finding it difficult to keep going. I have never liked the colour orange, but I couldn't get enough of it then. Colour, like sound, has its own vibration and we are naturally drawn towards the things that will help heal and balance.

Massage, aromatherapy and reflexology are all wonderful ways of getting you back together again, especially if you have been shocked 'out of your body'. T'ai chi, qui gong and yoga are other ways of helping you come back to your centre, and will do your soul more good than a workout at the gym, although movement of just about any kind will help your body release feelings locked inside. Look for workshops using Gabrielle Roth's Five Rhythms. These are five different types of music, each representing a different feeling from flowing to staccato through chaos to lyrical and stillness. Gabrielle Roth tells us to 'move your body to clear your mind', so as you let your body respond to the different rhythms your feelings are expressed through its movement. Better out than in, as the saying goes.

There are some other simple ways that you can help your body, which may be stating the obvious, but fresh air, energy-supplying food (as opposed to chocolate and chips) and drinking plenty of water to flush out the system can help you get stronger faster.

Help for the Mind

You may or may not feel like talking about this intense soulmate connection and the effects it's having or has had on you. But talking about it will help you begin to understand. It may not be easy to find a therapist who will help you see the spiritual implications of what has happened, but this is the point of it all. Exploring your past lives will certainly help to get a better perspective. Some people are nervous of stepping into these uncharted waters, so it's important that you find a fully qualified practitioner, who will not tell you about your past lives, but help you find out for yourself – the only truly valid form of discovery. A past life experience is not dissimilar to going into the Internet for information. Tap in www.mypastlives/soulmates, press the button and you find yourself in a 'field' of information, which is your own personal history. As Jalaluddin Rumi says so beautifully:

> *If you can't go somewhere,*
> *Move in the passageways of the self.*

The process of understanding and healing may take a little time, depending on how willing you are to let go of your old ideas and beliefs about yourself. It is in soulmate situations that we often wish we could look into a crystal ball and since we don't believe we can do this ourselves we go in search of psychics, sensitives, clairvoyants or tarot readers. Again, credibility of the person you consult is an imperative. One of the problems in looking for this sort of help is that we become selectively deaf and hear only what we want to hear. But if it is grief and loss you are coping with as a result of the death of a soulmate, there are psychics who specialise in what is known as 'evidence of survival'. This means they have the ability to become conduits for the one who has left earth to communicate with the one left behind. But results are never guaranteed and it may be that we have to come to terms with the fact that the loved other is either unable to or is not allowed to communicate.

Grief here on earth also binds the soul of the one who has left, so it is important to turn this event around somehow, knowing that they have not gone for ever, and you will meet again. But there are many documented examples of the loved one making their presence felt in little ways that also confirm that there is life after life. Many psychics have the ability to 'read' auras. In other words they get a sense of what is going on in your life by the colour and state of your auric field. So, if you decide to have such a consultation, be 'open' but let them supply you with the information and corroborative evidence that they are indeed in touch with another level of consciousness.

A tarot card reading can also be a valuable tool that will give you an overview of a difficult situation, and again you need to find a reputable and experienced interpreter of the cards. The tarot pack is a divinatory tool; in other words it is a way of accessing information without interference from the left-brain, logical mind. There are other, less complicated aids for helping, such as angel cards and the runes. Taking one of these on a daily basis can provide a mini compass through a wobbling time. Stating the intention 'What do I need today?' and, without looking, choosing a card or rune, you will find that the angels may produce 'Honesty' or 'Communication' and just this single word can help clarify your focus for the day. I have always found the runes extremely helpful if you want a bit more depth.

It may be that you just can't get this soulmate out of your head, and it begins to become obsessional. Round and round goes the mind, reliving situations, trying to work out solutions, wondering about endless 'what ifs'. Our minds need to be brought to heel in such a situation, as they can tie us in knots and we will not be able to see the wood for the trees. Stepping back from whomever and whatever it is that's driving you to distraction gives you a break rather than a breakdown. This requires a bit of discipline so perhaps you can give yourself an allotted time every day to indulge obsessive thoughts and feelings, and then get on with your life. This gives the mind the sense that it is not being totally ignored, but cannot run and ruin your life.

Consulting a good and reputable karmic astrologer can also be an extremely illuminating experience that will help cast light on the forces that are at work. Magazine astrology bears no resemblance to having your own natal chart drawn up and interpreted. Astrology is not predictive – it won't tell you whether there is a future in this relationship or not, but it is an enormously valuable tool for helping to understand our emotional weather based on the ingredients that make up our personality. Having your own chart drawn up with your soulmate's can help you see what works and where the challenges are. The added dimension of karma revealed by the chart provides insights into the history of lifetimes that may have been spent together working through a particular theme.

The planets in the heavens will not tell us *what* is going to happen any more than our sun sign tells us *who* we are. We are all made up of the same stuff as each other, but the proportion of ingredients one to another is what gives us our personality traits. A birth chart is like opening a packet of seeds that shows you the possibilities and potential contained within you and the sort of 'weather' you are likely to experience during the planting and growing of the seeds, if you choose to plant them. There can be no other who will have *exactly* the same chart as you, unless they were born in exactly the same place at exactly the same time. This is your own unique blueprint in all its splendour, like your DNA and fingerprint, which shows all the possibilities and potential available in your specific packet. All the seeds will not necessarily flower, but by taking a close look we can get an idea of our potential.

Your sun sign does not *make* you a Virgo, Leo or Scorpio, but is a celestial symbol for what needs to be attained in this lifetime – a skin that may be grown into. It also represents what is at the heart of you and, because it symbolises the active or yang side of your personality, provides the drive for you to realise the positive attributes of your sign.

The moon, on the other hand, will be placed in a different sign at the time of your birth and stands for the yin or hidden, emotional aspects of your personality. While the sun pushes us to strive for differentiation, the moon wants to have its emotional needs met and to merge with another. Your sun sign speaks of your active, decision-making abilities, while the moon tells of your basic, instinctive needs.

The placement of each of the planets in your birth chart will then expand the portrait of your personality, adding more ingredients to the basic recipe. Mercury, for example, is the smallest and fastest planet in our solar system and where it is placed in your chart gives a clue about your ability to comprehend and communicate, your need to understand things and asks whether you will recognise the interconnectedness of everything, or just be a bank full of data.

We have all heard that men come from Mars and women from Venus, but the placement of these two planets in our charts will give us clues about our own masculine and feminine attributes. The popularity of books on this subject suggests that we are aware of these two opposites, but they are internal rather than external. We may be living in a woman's body but we need to understand the masculine aspect of ourselves, as a man needs to understand and accept his femininity without feeling he will become a homosexual in the process. The ancient astrological glyphs for these two planets are now used as biological symbols for male and female. As the sun and moon represent father and mother, here we have Mars as the conqueror and Venus the lover. Their positioning in our chart is particularly interesting in that they reveal what we look for in our 'opposite number' – or rather those qualities that we require ourselves, but need to have them reflected back in order for us to own them in ourselves.

Jupiter explains our need to experience the divine, our

religious urge. Remember that the word religion stems from the Latin *re ligare*, to reunite. Saturn and the other planets represent the other ingredients that broadly define our personalities, and for those of us who need the world to tell us about ourselves this is helpful. The more we understand the mechanisms that motivate us, the easier it is to identify and rectify what appears to be engine failure.

The placement of the planets in our own individual charts will be in the various zodiacal signs and will help us identify which of the four types, relating to the four elements, we fall into. In order to understand this more fully, you will need your chart in front of you which will tell you what houses (signs) the planets were in when you were born. So although your sun may be in the watery sign of Cancer, you may have a preponderance of planets in earth or air, which will temper the effect of the wateriness – symbolising emotions – of your personality.

These four elements then are air (thinking), and its opposite, water (feeling); and earth (sensation) and its opposite, fire (intuition). Air represents our thinking function and Gemini, Libra and Aquarius would rather think through something than rely on their feelings, as their opposites do, the watery, feeling signs of Pisces, Scorpio and Cancer. Water sign people value personal relationships and human values above all else, and are often in touch with the darker side of human nature, which earns them their reputation for compassion and empathy.

Earthy people – those whose sun and most of their planets are in Taurus, Capricorn and Virgo – rely on their senses to interpret the world, and are often known for their practicality, efficiency and common sense but may suffer from lack of vision. The fire signs – Aries,

Leo and Sagittarius – are intuitives, which means they seem to have an uncanny knack of grasping the undercurrents at work in a situation. They have strong 'hunches' about things, which often prove unerringly accurate. The downside of being predominantly fiery can mean a horror of routine, self-centredness or ill-tempered individualism.

These very basic astrological facts have been included because you may be, as I am, a watery Pisces but with most of my planets in air, which means I do more thinking than feeling. My head found it extremely helpful to discover that my soulmate and I had 'come through time and space to meet at this point, in order to resolve an ancient karmic situation' in all its ramifications, most of which were about plunging me into the depths of my feelings. Astrology is a fascinating and detailed science, whether you are fiery, watery, earthy or intuitive, and it's worth finding a good astrologer to explore the history of your soulmate's link with your own soul.

All the foregoing will help calm the storm in your aura that's been created by a soulmate, the bottom line of which is all about . . .

Help for the Soul

Whether you face a difficult soulmate on a daily basis, are subjected to sporadic encounters, or are trying to recover from such a meeting, it is your soul who is pressing you to make contact. The trouble with deep emotional pain is that it cuts us off from the very source of what will help us heal. As Rumi says:

We are pain and what cures pain.

It is as if our switchboards lose all their connections to life, our energy field becomes contracted and we are just a tight ball. While there are no quick fixes for this situation, paradoxically the cure is only a thought away. Because where *is* the soul in all of this? Deep wounding has the potential to make you a victim for the rest of your life, not living, but existing – or to ask yourself what you have learned about your self through this experience. This lifetime is a one-act play, a soul drama, and the person (or people) who is responsible for your difficulties is another soul playing its part, as you are. But we have got so involved with our scripts and roles that we have forgotten the fact that we, like them, are 'acting out' the drama. This shift in focus already starts to put your soul in the driving seat.

Since soulmates tend to scramble our vibes, and we know from Chapter 1 that the vibration of the soul is finer and faster than the other layers of our subtle anatomy (thoughts and emotions), we need to calm down first of all. Easier said than done when jealousy is tearing your heart out, anger has got you by the throat, or you are sickened by guilt, remorse or betrayal. But sometimes, even in the middle of wild emotional weather, we can hear the still, small voice of our soul. It's like arriving in the eye of a storm where there is an almost eerie calm and stillness. There are various ways we can help ourselves find this still point of the soul. There is music for a start. This is another form of vibrational 'medicine', which has the ability to soothe our ruffled airwaves, lift our spirit and help us settle down. Sitting by a river, by the sea, on a mountaintop or with your back against a tree can also have a wonderfully restorative effect. Putting yourself in a natural environment is food for the soul. You might discover gardening therapy; getting your hands in the soil and watching things grow helps the soul come down to earth and us to get out of our heads. Take some time out by yourself, and see what that feels like. It's not always possible to see the wood for the trees when we are standing in the middle of the forest and *all* relationships benefit from space.

Sitting in a church, temple or some other structure where people have communicated with a divine force through the ages can also bring a sense of calm and gives us the chance to hear, or rather feel the presence of our soul. From this contact we will feel encouraged to walk on. Lighting a candle and making an inner statement that with this candle you acknowledge the light your soul can shine on your life helps to establish the link to your soul.

Prayer and meditation are other ways that we can bring the soul into being, and to use its powerful wisdom to illuminate a soulmate (or any other) situation. This is about spirituality, not religion, and even if we never go to a church or temple we may find ourselves sending up supplications in moments of dire distress. 'Please, God, take away this pain and I promise I'll be good for the rest of my life,' is the little girl or boy striking a bargain with 'someone' who has the power and ability to sort things out. By opening to your own soul, you link with your own power to heal and sort things out. Praying is like transmitting a message from your self to your Self, while meditation is more receptive. A meditative state can be evoked anywhere, once you've got the hang of it.

In the meantime, a little ritual will help put the ego/personality on notice that this is soul time. Ritual and ceremony are practices we have lost in our contemporary lives, unfortunately. Rites of passage, so crucial to acknowledging and moving us through the stages of life, have been reduced to the hatches, matches and despatches moments. Making a certain place your own little sanctuary by placing a candle, a flower, a stone you have collected from the beach, perhaps some incense and a cushion to sit on only requires a small corner of your living space. But you are telling your soul that you will give it at least a small corner of your life to give it time and attention. Using the little sanctuary to listen to music, meditate or contemplate builds up an energy that becomes easier and easier to tap in to every time you sit there. A Muslim is reminded five times a day to be aware of Allah. If we could remind ourselves even once a day of the presence of our souls, our lives would take on a different flavour.

Drawing and painting are another way of helping the soul. It's not about trying to produce something you can put on the wall, but just using colour and line to 'say' something that the voice box is unable to express. Try using your non-dominant hand to free this communication even further from the dictator in the left brain, who just wants results. Or working with clay may suit you better.

As we become more aware of our connection to our soul, it may become more and more appropriate to sever the connections (at an earthly level) with a soulmate. As already explained, what happens between soulmates is the result of the initial 'recognition' and connection created by the tuning fork effect, which generates a resonance. Our energy fields then engage with one another and, more specifically, lines of energy will link our chakras. Hence the feeling of 'heart to heart' or 'mind to mind', but it can be (and often is) a matter of throat to throat (communication) and solar plexus to solar plexus (power) or, in the case of a sexual soulmate, sacral to sacral. These links are like cords between you, and the more intense the connection, the stronger the cord, which can even be felt physically. Cutting these invisible ties with a soulmate will help you to free yourself, and also give you more energy to do other things.

It has been said that a problem cannot be solved at the level at which it exists, and the following guided visualisation gives you a means of taking those soulmate relationships to a place where the solution is easier to access, a place where you can effectively cut the ties that are holding you back. You might like to record it on to a tape and then play it to yourself, or get someone to read it to you. Before starting any meditation, make sure you are sitting in a comfortable position and that you are not going to be disturbed.

Cutting the Ties

Begin by taking some deep, easy breaths and begin to relax; take the air right down to your belly, and let the tension go. Holding tension uses energy and there are other, more interesting ways to use this energy.

As you sit here, quiet and relaxed, letting the tension in your body drain away into the floor, imagine for a moment that you hear a gentle knock on the door.

Using the power of your mind, imagine that you leave your chair to go and see who it might be, knocking gently, but firmly on the door.

There is a sense of anticipation, as you approach the door,

---

to open it; and as you open it, you are aware of an incredible light. This light surrounds a being, the being who was knocking gently on your door. This being may have the form of an angel, or some other wise person. You know that this being is wise and compassionate and wants only to support and guide you. It is as if you know this being, you feel totally safe and comfortable in their presence.

Then you notice that behind this being of light there is a golden staircase, to which you are gently guided by the hand of this wise being. And you both begin to ascend; perhaps it feels as if you are almost floating up this staircase, up and up, until you arrive at a place where there is some kind of seat. Notice what kind of seat this is: it may be simple, or it may be more like a throne. Whatever it looks like, know that this is your own, personal seat, so go and sit in it now, and notice how it feels. You are aware of the presence of your wise being, or angel, still close at hand, but now it is as if you can look down on the earth far below you.

Now focus your mind on this person who is bothering you. Invite that person to come up the stairs to meet you as you sit in your place of power; focus on your heart chakra and allow the words to come from here. Say whatever it is you feel you need to say to them, but have been unable to either because they have not listened in the past, or you have not had the courage to do so. You are speaking from the heart now, and the heart of the other receives what comes from the heart.

Allow time for your words to be felt and heard.

Notice the response in the other person as you communicate with them from this place of your own soul power. Perhaps you feel there are some energy cords that exist between you, which you would like to release? Where in your body are these cords attached? Notice in which of the seven chakras you may feel this cording that it is now time to release and imagine that, using a pair of silver scissors, you now cut these ties that bind you together. Perhaps you may even feel or sense something in your body as this cord is cut. Again, using the power of your mind, and knowing that energy follows thought, imagine that your end of this cord is drawn back into the chakra that it came from, and seal it with white light. Repeat this procedure with any other cords between you and this person that are no longer appropriate.

2–3 MINUTES' SILENCE

When you feel that the energy between you and this person is clear it will be time for them to return down the staircase to the physical plane. Let them go. And then take a few moments sitting calmly in your seat of power, aware of the presence of that wise person or being of light.

You have been looking, as it were, down on the earthly plane from this place above the earth. Now imagine that this seat of yours has the ability to turn 180 degrees to face in the opposite direction. Notice how easily your seat turns gently round to look at what has been behind you for the last little while. Now you are aware of the levels above and beyond; notice the quality of light that there is here, perhaps a strong sense of love and support. Spend a few moments exploring this space now.

SILENCE for 3 or 4 MINUTES

Now it is time to turn your seat around again and to begin your descent down the staircase and back into the physical realms, knowing that this place is always there, only a thought away, if you want to resolve something with someone, or if you need to take yourself to a place where you can see things from a different perspective. A place where you can also remember that there is more than a physical reality, and you are more than a body and personality.

Find yourself back in the room where you started this journey. And now become aware of the sounds around you, wriggle your fingers and toes and then take a deep breath. When you are ready, open your eyes and stand up and stretch.

As our bodies, minds and souls come together and begin to work as the team they were meant to be, it's as if we begin to stand in the centre of ourselves, like being in the axis of a wheel, rather than out of control somewhere on the rim. As we begin to understand what seem to be problematical soulmate relationships – how and why they affect us – a major shift in perspective takes place. We move from naming, blaming and being victims or controllers to realising that we are all individuals in our own right, not products of our family, culture or religion. We live in a jungle, and will come across all sorts of creatures who also have a right to be whom and what they are. We have no idea what anyone else's karmic script is or who, at a soul level, has taken on the difficult roles of extreme soulmates. What would have happened if there hadn't been a Judas Iscariot? The world stage throws up those souls who change collective history in the same way that our own personal soulmates do: by pressing our buttons and giving us the opportunity to move in to the energy of the heart.

the heart of the matter
What's It All About?

Those who don't feel this Love
Pulling them like a river,
Those who don't drink dawn
Like a cup of springwater
Or take in sunset like supper,
Those who don't want to change,
Let them sleep.

JALALUDDIN RUMI

The purpose of this book has been to take a long, deep look at the business of soulmates, in order to blow away some cobwebs of illusion and delusion that have wrapped themselves round our hearts and minds concerning mythical partners. There may have been some dreams shattered along the way and perhaps there are those who *have* experienced a deep and permanent loving relationship who might feel this is a cynical view. They are fortunate that in this incarnation their souls have given themselves the opportunity to learn through loving and being loved.

My point is not to say that such relationships don't exist, but they are the exception rather than the rule, and life must not be put on hold while you wait for this to happen;

nor should you quietly die inside as the years pass and that magical other doesn't appear, or alternatively seems to have moved through your life like a flash flood, and then vanished. You may not have experienced true love – yet – in your life, according to the happily ever after myth, but that ecstatic feeling of joy and love is like a seed that exists inside us all. Why wait to have it watered by a gardener who may never appear – in this lifetime, anyway?

Perhaps you'd like to pause for a moment, close your eyes and imagine yourself in a garden. And when you are there, just notice what sort of garden it is, whether there are walls and fences around it, whether it is orderly or unkempt and if there are flowers and trees. Perhaps it needs a little wildness somewhere to bring it back to life? Perhaps it looks as if people have come in and trampled on it, pruned the shrubs too hard, or there has been storm damage. Never mind, somewhere in the heart of it you'll find this perfect flower, because somewhere in *everyone's* garden is the flower of the soul. It may be found buried in a tangle of undergrowth, or trying to grow in an orderly bed of roses where it keeps on getting cut back because it doesn't quite 'fit'. But it is there. Sometimes this garden of yours needs to be closed to the public, so that it can restore itself in peace and quiet. The seasons need to be observed, too. So there are times when it seems as if there are no leaves on the trees, or flowers anywhere. But that's because things are happening on the *in*side, unseen and in the dark. It's gestation time. There are days when the gate to the garden must be closed so that you can walk in it alone, and enjoy that solitude, listen to what it might want to tell you, and tend that one incredible flower that is at the heart of the garden.

Getting to the Heart of It

The heart of anything will always hold the key to deeper understanding, and for us humans it is this key that will unlock another mystery, and that mystery is encapsulated in the four-letter word, love. Love goes hand in hand with hearts. It waits to take us beyond all our *samskaras*, our karmic backlog, our deep insecurities, our expectations, our ego and personality dramas and disappointments. *It is the theme behind every other single soul theme.* One of the problems we have is with the word itself, which can be used to describe everything from the mundane to the deeply spiritual. Eskimos have over twenty different words to describe the nature of snow, because precise understanding of the quality of snow is vital to an Eskimo's survival. Even the Greeks have four words to describe the different aspects of love. The fact that we can produce only one word to express the feeling we may have for our favourite TV soap, verse from a sacred text, our grandmother or cat, speaks reams. Our understanding of love can come only through our *hearts*. Why don't I love someone with all my liver?

In these days of transplants, the fact that the heart has its own intelligence has been demonstrated many times by the stories of transplantees, who tell of feeling the presence of their donor. A born-again Christian woke up swearing and cursing after receiving the heart of a raunchy biker; a woman who had received the heart of a sailor killed in a boating accident found that her terror of water had vanished, and she had a great desire to go sailing and swimming. The possibilities of what may happen if, God forbid, we start to use animal organs is better left alone.

Not a good idea for anyone who already snores and grunts, perhaps.

What an extraordinary creature the heart is! It can weep, sink, race, faint, flutter, burn, harden, burst, melt, rejoice, stop or fail. It can be broken, frozen, lost, warmed, touched or turned to stone. It may be a lonely hunter, or like a gazelle (or even hart?) leaping and almost flying, but in the heart of the heart you will always find courage, strength, gentleness, vulnerability and compassion.

Your heart may be made of gold or ice but, whatever it is, it's clearly not just a mechanical pump. Zooming in on our hearts reveals that it has a multi-dimensional nature. On the physical level, it beats 4,200 times an hour. Its four chambers take in old tired blood from the body's circuitry and send it off to the lungs to be reinspired. The left side receives the new blood back from the lungs and then pushes it out (2,000 gallons a day) through 60,000 miles of tubes with a force strong enough to reach the capillaries in the big toe. It literally keeps us going moment by moment and when it stops, we are gone within minutes. It not only keeps us alive by moving our life force round, but also allows us to know about that other life force: love. Knowing about love is as important as keeping us alive, unless we opt for a half-hearted, heartless life. Hearts need to rejoice, to sing, to fly. They need to *love*. And if they get broken by grief, wounded, rejected or pierced by love's arrows, it may feel as if some form of death is imminent, but that death is the possibility of the heart's doors permanently closing. These are the times to be tender with our hearts, and ensure that they stay open in spite of the pain. A hardened heart has closed its doors to love, and therefore life itself.

Soulmates

Hearts are for giving. They have the courage to take us into the depths of our feelings. They are the place where heaven and earth come together; body and soul embrace each other here, in the centre of our chests. The Sanskrit symbol for the heart chakra is a six-pointed star, sometimes known as the Star of David. It is a universal symbol representing two triangles, one pointing down (heaven coming to earth) and the other pointing up (earth to heaven). So if our hearts are the meeting ground for heaven and earth, and are the seats of our soul, how could we possibly be half-hearted about love?

Historical Hearts

The heart has a history of being understood as the seat of the soul, starting with the ancient Egyptians. It's still a mystery how their sophisticated knowledge of mathematics, architecture, astrology and medicine came into being and flourished in such a relatively short space of time. But there is no doubt about the fact that they knew that the heart was a crucial compass for life on earth, and believed it to have its own intelligence.

My heart ticks in my chest like a beetle . . .
It resonates like the bow string of an archer. It hums like the
String of a lyre. Love. Love. Give me love, sibilant love,
*   thundering love.*
It is myself that speaks to my heart, my ka, my double.
The heart leaps and answers to its name.
Its words are the deeds of my body. Its deeds have been my
*   own thoughts;*
Its blood the fluid of gods, river of joy and sadness.

The heart of the matter

Said Normandi Ellis in her beautiful translation of *The Egyptian Book of the Dead*:

'Think with your heart and feel with your mind' was the maxim that would lead, after death, to each person's heart being placed on the scales of Ma'at to be weighed against the feather of truth and integrity. If the heart was heavy, further incarnations were required until it became as light as the feather. The quality of an Egyptian pharaoh's rule and a magician's magic was said to be directly linked to the quality of his heart. The Sixth Dynasty Egyptian scribe and sage, Ptahhotep, advised his son to

> Follow your heart and desire as long as you live. Do not more than is asked. Shorten not the time of following your heart. It is a sin to encroach upon its time. Take no care daily beyond the maintenance of your house. When wealth comes, still follow your heart, for riches are nothing when the heart is glum.

Since the beginning of time there have been those who have known the ways of love, spiritual masters who taught how to activate and water the latent seed within each of our hearts. They knew how to awaken this power, this longing that the soul has for its beloved. Following in Egyptian footsteps, Christians and Islamic Sufis used the wounded and the winged heart respectively as symbols for something deeply divine. The pierced and bleeding sacred heart of Jesus is always healing, but never healed, since the wound is the gateway to heaven and must remain for ever open. For Muslims, a clean heart is like a mirror, reflecting the light of Allah. The heart makes constant appearances in Islamic and mystical Sufi poetry and texts.

Sufism came into being as a reaction to the degeneration of Islam as it spread wider and wider and became, like Christianity, bigoted and under the control of a few. The Sufis, like their Christian counterparts, the Gnostics, kept the fire of this divine love burning through the centuries and were persecuted and annihilated because of it. Our search for the beloved, a soulmate, that other who will know us better than we know ourselves, is the soul asking us to look for love.

Heart and Soul

This journey to find love is the one referred to and eulogised by the Sufi mystics. As the Islamic saying states: 'The Sufis understand with the heart what cannot be understood with the head.' It is the journey of the soul.

> *O servant where dost thou seek me?*
> *Lo! I am beside thee. I am neither in the temple nor in the*
>   *mosque,*
> *Neither am I in rites and ceremonies,*
> *Nor in yoga nor in renunciation.*
> *If thou art a true seeker, thou shalt at once see me.*
> *Thou shalt meet me in a moment's time*
> KABIR

Ultimately nothing else has any consequence. They are speaking of a journey to find a love that will not be found in the physical arms of another. This love belongs to a Beloved with a capital 'B'. It is a love that transcends all others, the ultimate love, the love into which we may disappear and lose all sense of our earthbound personality and identity. Sufis say that we are all students in the School of Love. They know that love is the most powerful and active force in the universe, and that it cannot be compared with anything else. We know this in our heart of hearts. Why else would the words of a thirteenth-century Muslim, of Afghan origin – Jalaluddin Rumi – make him the most popular poet in the world today? Rumi's words hit us like telegrams from some divine source that we know about, but have forgotten. Our hearts leap and swoon as the words rise from the page to tell us about the burning, passionate madness of the lover for the Beloved.

> *Whatever I have said about Love*
> *When Love comes, I am ashamed to speak.*
> JALALUDDIN RUMI

The love that he speaks of is the love of the soul for God, Allah, the Creator, the source, the One or whatever name you want to give to that power that, bafflingly, simply is. He reminds us of the unlived sorrow of separation, the uncontainable joy of union, of the limitless horizon of the heart and the desire of this heart to find its true friend.

Rumi's timeless – and timely – messages speak directly from his heart to our own. His words have the ring of truth born of experiece – his own experience. He was a professor of theology who, on his way home from school one day (in 1244), met a ragged dervish named Shams of Tabriz. According to the story, Shams recited this verse to him:

> *If knowledge does not liberate the self from the self,*
> *Then ignorance is better than such knowledge*

It was as if Shams had touched some deep truth in Rumi's heart. He fell at the dervish's feet, and from that moment a furnace of love burned in Rumi for Shams, who then one day disappeared, perhaps sensing the jealousy that their relationship had created with Rumi's students and family. Rumi heard that he was in Damascus, and sent one of his sons to bring him back. Once more Rumi fell at his feet, overwhelmed by the joy of their passionate and ecstatic reunion. They became inseparable, but again jealousy from his students and younger son ended the meeting of these two souls – and this time it was permanent. Shams was murdered, and Rumi was sent spinning down into the deepest well of grief, lost and alone in his ocean of love.

This was his epiphany. He realised that the overwhelming love, passion and grief he was feeling belonged, not to Shams, but to a Beloved more magnificent, more compassionate, more powerful than any human being – the divine itself. His love, and loss, of Shams was the key to his understanding of divine love and the inspiration for his writings. Rumi's words have fanned the flame of this love in modern times, creating a forest fire. The fact that he was a Muslim also points the way through the quagmire of current assumptions about Islam based on terrorists, *jihads*, fundamentalists and weapons of mass destruction. It shows us that at the heart of it all the routes we take on our different journeys all arrive at the same destination. This love is of the highest order. It does not create division or separation, it recognises that we are all human and get things wrong before we get them right. It is not a love born from fear or hope, but a love inspired by the magnificence, the beauty of vast infinity and the detail of a moth's wing or the sound of a grey dove:

I was sleeping, and being comforted
By a cool breeze, when suddenly a grey dove
From a thicket sang and sobbed with longing,
And reminded me of my own passion.

I had been away from my own soul so long,
So late-sleeping, but that dove's crying
*Woke me and made me cry **Praise***
To all early-waking grievers!
ADI AL-RIGA

The Invisible Lover

But loving someone who is everywhere and nowhere is a challenge to say the least, and most of us have probably only fleetingly glimpsed through the keyhole of its implications. At our current level of understanding, love needs an object, because perhaps the most important part of love, the part that will endure for us as human beings, is friendship. I can't sit down with God, have a cup of tea and chew over the difficulties and challenges of being human because there seems to be no input, no sharing. If I can't *touch* this being of love and feel its presence, how can I know it's really there? Rumi understands this when he says:

Today, like every other day, we wake up empty
And frightened. Don't open the door to the study and
Begin reading. Take down a musical instrument.
Let the beauty we love be what we do.
There are hundreds of ways to kneel and kiss the ground.

167

Soulmates

Perhaps it is not such an impossible task, after all. Allah is nearer to us than our jugular vein, states the Qur'an, a book that is actually what we would call these days a 'channelled' work. Our Beloved is beside us, in us and around us, but we have forgotten how to notice its presence, in the same way that we are not aware of our hearts beating in our chests. Our search for our soulmates in human form is our soul's search for the Beloved. It is as if our human lovers are cardboard cutouts for the divine. We know that there is this other somewhere, out there. The truth of the matter is that it is not *out* there, but *in* here after all, and our hearts, like Rumi's, can be the receivers of divine telegrams informing us of this love. When our eyes start to open from our deep slumber and this remembering begins to happen, we begin to see a different world. Something like the homecoming of the prodigal son . . .

> When a world finishes and time runs out,
> The sleepers awaken.
> They discover the meaning of love,
> The depth of their eternal nature.
> They find meaning in every second.
> For many people in our world, the time has come to remember.
> SAMUEL SAGAN

Hearts and Minds

Since we are not all Rumis or Kabirs and have been educated to trust facts rather than feelings, there is information available that may help you change your mind about your heart.

A non-profit-making organisation in the US, called the Institute of HeartMath, was set up over a decade ago to investigate and find a solution for the rising levels of personal stress experienced by people throughout the globe. They have been studying the effects that 'mismanaged' emotions have on every aspect of our life and producing educational packages for children, institutions and corporations to help people learn more about their hearts and minds, how to manage their emotions and thus reduce stress. Their work has grown out of earlier research showing that the heart appeared to be sending meaningful messages to the brain that were not only understood, but obeyed. A small band of cardiovascular researchers and neurophysiologists amalgamated their work which is now known as neurocardiology; study of the heart brain.

Their leading-edge research is focused on the relationship between the heart and the brain, and the ways in which this relationship affects us physically, mentally and emotionally. Their bio-medical findings have revealed that the heart is a 'highly complex, self organized processing centre with its own functioning "brain"'. At the HeartMath Research Center they demonstrate how the messages from the heart affect not only our physiology, but profoundly influence perception, emotions, behaviour, performance and health. They have discovered that when we experience feelings such as appreciation, love, care and compassion, there are clear changes in the patterns of activity in the autonomic nervous system, immune and hormone systems, the brain and the heart itself.

They have revealed that the heart and brain carry on a two-way dialogue, each influencing the other's functioning. 'Our research is exploring the influence of the heart's output on brain activity, emotional perception, experience and cognitive performance. We have shown that emotion-related changes in the heart's rhythmic activity are correlated with distinct changes in these variables. Our findings point to a link between positive emotions and improved cognitive functioning.' They also tell us that their research has revealed that the heart produces by far the most powerful rhythmic electromagnetic field in the body, and this field changes measurably according to the different emotions being experienced. The heart's electrical field is about 60 times greater than that of the brain, and its magnetic field more than 5,000 times larger. This heart field not only envelops every cell of the body, but also extends out in all directions. It can actually be measured several feet away from the body.

Their years of innovative scientific investigation have produced empirical evidence on the heart's central role in our feeling experiences. Now they have also proved that the electromagnetic signal produced by our hearts registers on the brain waves of those around us and is a key mediator of energy exchanges between people. In fact our hearts are actually chatting to each other – a heart-to-heart conversation – whenever we are engaged energetically with somebody. The HeartMath Institute has also proved the existence of that link between positive emotions and improved brainpower. So the ancient Egyptians with their 'Think with the heart and feel with the mind' knew exactly what they were talking about.

The heart has its reasons, that reason does not know.
PASCAL

Our computerised lives with digital everything have taken our ears away from birdsong and our eyes from observing the seasons. We have been blanked out, dumbed down and switched off to the astonishing world created *for* us, by the plastic world we have created for ourselves.

Conversations with the Beloved

But whether we like it or not, something is going on in our chest cavities of which we may not be consciously aware. I've already mentioned the collective outpourings in response to events such as Princess Diana's death. But there are other signs that our hearts are dying to be opened. Apart from the extraordinary popularity of the Islamic poets, many of our little everyday hearts have been touched by the writings of a man called Neale Donald Walsch. His series of books, called *Conversations with God*, have brought that Beloved, spoken of by the mystics, into our kitchens, our bedrooms and our daily lives. Through these books we find that the Beloved *is* as close to us as our jugular vein; not remote, sitting on a throne somewhere up there in the sky and wagging a judgemental finger at his naughty children, but right here with a heartstopping depth of wisdom, understanding and – oh yes! – love.

Neale Donald Walsch's conversations with God have changed the lives of literally millions of people because, simply put, the heart recognises a truth when it hears one. Again, 'What comes from the heart is heard by the heart.' 'Aha!' says the heart, 'I know that – but somehow I have forgotten.' Neale Donald Walsch has said of his books that his only regret is the fact that the title includes the phrase 'An Uncommon Dialogue'. Since publishing (over

4 million copies), he has received countless letters from people everywhere telling of their own experience of writing to a higher power and receiving an answer that could not have come from the personality.

Heartfelt Letters

Perhaps you would like to try this for yourself, and see what happens. In my workshops on Soulmates, and the Power of Love, we make a connection to the heart by closing the eyes and going inside the body. As you gently approach your heart from the inside, you get a sense of the state it's in. Then we draw what has been observed. It's literally heart-rending to see the images people produce of weeping, broken, battered, defended and tiny little hearts. Having done this, we then, in the style of Neale Donald Walsch, write a letter to our heart, which might go something like this one, which I wrote to my own after going through a false-alarm heart attack:

> *Dear Heart,*
>
> *I am sorry that I pushed you to the limits. I'm afraid I never learned about limits – as you have discovered. I didn't mean to jeopardise your steadfast support, perhaps the only stable rhythm in the chaos of my life at the moment. I will listen to your eternal wisdom, for I know that it is you who holds the key that opens the door to my soul. You, who have a foot in both worlds, are like a quiet, wise teacher, never intruding or demanding, but always standing behind the child as she stumbles through life. Ticking away in my chest, holding the secrets of my heartfelt moments deep within you, you have never failed me – even in my moments*

of terror. But I feel you flutter these days. What do you wish to say? Have you lost the heart to go on? You have opened your arms to embrace others' hearts and not always found responses. You have crossed your arms akimbo and refused to let some in – I wonder how you decide? I know some of the things that touch you – a wren's song, a fern unfolding, water running over stones and Eva Cassidy's voice – but there must be so much more. I know you love solitude but sing when you are with my sons, my friends and in those moments of speechless laughter.

I am sorry you had to take such drastic action to make me pay attention to what you have to say. I'm good at telling everybody else to listen to their hearts, and pay little attention to you, my own.

I do love you . . .

Sue

My heart had the grace to reply:

Dear Sue,

It seems you have heard me at last. I am sorry for those heart-stopping moments, but it seemed the only way I could truly get your attention. I hope I won't need to do it again. No, I won't stop beating for a while yet, because there is work to be done, and although there have been times when you hoped I'd let you off the hook by simply giving up – that is not the way. It seems difficult for you to grasp the fact that I am full of love – I have an endless supply – but you keep opening and shutting my doors, believing that the granaries of my love are somehow at risk or will run dry. What a notion! Does the sun stop rising, the trees growing or babies smiling? By the way, it is not I who separate the *lovable from the unlovable. All are children of the One with hearts of their own – smothered, defended, frozen or ignored perhaps, but always present, patiently waiting for love to arrive or, rather, to be released. There is an eternal nature to some things and that includes me. The love that I am capable of is beyond your understanding. It is so vast and so splendid – sometimes like a firework display of breathtaking colour and design, sometimes deeper and stiller than the deepest ocean, wider than the widest horizon and as mysterious as the night sky. Don't be afraid of this, but please do stop thinking so small. The pain I feel has more to do with the fact that you let that head of yours rule me. I don't want to be ruled – nor will I – by a fearful dictator who has truly no idea of the magnitude of my abilities.*

I am, after all, the voice of your soul, and have the ear of the One who loves you beyond all others. I dare you to cross the threshold, just for a moment, and feel the power, strength and tenderness of the love that I have for you. I may take up only a small space in your body, but I can hold all of you in the palm of my hand. I can fly to other realms, too – all these things I can do, and more, as the saying goes, and as you will discover. I have had to remind you of my presence by making you feel as if I was being crushed, which is how I felt, but now perhaps you'll let me love you in the way that, truly, you deserve. This love of which I speak is not of the planet earth, but has its source in the eternal wellspring of life, if I can put it like that. This means it can encompass all worlds and yet be delighted, as you know, by the wren's song outside your window – her little tiny body bursting with all that sound.

I have said enough for now. Keep in touch.

Your ever-loving Heart

After receiving a letter from your heart, you may realise – as I did – that you have found a friend who has been beside you all along. We sometimes forget, with old faithful friends, how much they love and support us, as we search in the faces of others for what must first be found in our selves. Which brings us full circle to soulmates, or, as T.S. Eliot says in one of his *Four Quartets*:

> We shall not cease from exploration
> And the end of all our exploring
> Will be to arrive where we started
> And know the place for the first time.

Happily Ever After, After All

The importance of soulmates is in giving us the opportunity to let go of all those feelings that stand in the way of love. Difficult soulmates are truly polishing the heart's lantern. They ask us to move beyond the *samskaras*, the past (and present) life dramas, all the issues of the chakras that bog us down and to move to the heart of our hearts, where there is no fear. It's not easy to replace fear with love, as many contemporary teachers urge us to do. So begin with the first step in moving up the ladder of love, by trusting – trusting that there is an order and purpose to everything under the sun – and once trust is in place, it becomes easier to move towards our relationship with our real Beloved. This will have a knock-on effect on everything in your life, as the institute of HeartMath has discovered.

Everybody loves a lover, in this case a lover of life. The more we just let go of the issues we have with other people and realise that they are actually reflecting something back to us about ourselves, the quicker our 'note' changes pitch. Our inner tuning fork no longer resonates with soulmates who will bring the contents of our shadow into focus, but will attract those who reflect our change of heart. A clear, clean heart sings out. That note is heard and will be responded to.

We are now ready for a relationship that is sacred. Our intense connections with others of every shape and size have been a preparation for this. Like a bride being prepared for her wedding, we have been scrubbed, polished and dusted perhaps by one, or perhaps by a team of soulmates who, even though they were not consciously aware of the plan, were vital to this preparation.

A sacred relationship, like a sacred space, must be entered into with reverence, because it is a place where we may become consciously aware of something that is beyond our everyday selves. Divorce statistics tell us that our relationships are not working and something needs to change. That something is our understanding of what is really going on, because in these 'new' relationships only the truth will work. Being scrupulously honest with ourselves about ourselves changes the reflections we find of ourselves in those with whom we have close contact. Realising that intense and difficult relationships are our soulmates helping us (and themselves) prepare for a union that is beyond our imagination moves our perspective from ant to eagle. These soulmates are there to help clear the weeds on that path in your garden which leads to the amazing flower at the heart of it all: your self.

I hope that the journey through the contents of this book have given you some clues that will take you into

the amazing mystery of your self and lead you to that
ecstatic union with your Beloved.

> *Work of the eyes is done. Now go and do the heart-work.*
> RAINER MARIA RILKE

bibliography

Avery, Jeanne, *Astrology & Your Past Lives* (Simon & Schuster)

Barks, Coleman, *The Essential Rumi* (Penguin)

Barks, Coleman and Michael Green, *The Illuminated Rumi* (Broadway Books)

Braden, Gregg, *Awakening to Zero Point* (Radio Bookstore Press)

Braden, Gregg, *Walking Between the Worlds: The Science of Compassion* (Radio Bookstore Press)

Carroll, Lee and Jan Tober, *The Indigo Children* (Hay House)

Cott, Jonathan, *The Search for Omm Seti* (A. A. Gaddis)

Davis, Dr Brenda, *Journey of the Soul* (Hodder Mobius)

Ellis, Normandi, *Dreams of Isis* (Quest Books)

Gerber, Dr Richard, *Vibrational Medicine for the 21st Century* (Piatkus)

Greene, Liz, *Relating* (Coventure)

Greene, Liz and Juliet Sharman-Burke, *The Mythic Journey* (Gothic Image)

Griffiths, Bede, *A New Vision of Reality* (Fount)

Hall, Judy, *The Way of Karma* (Thorsons)

Hall, Judy, *Hands Across Time* (Findhorn Press)

Hall, Judy, *Astrology & Your Past Lives* (Godsfield)

Hand Clow, Barbara, *Catastrophobia* (Bear & Company)

Hardo, Trutz, *Children Who Have Lived Before* (CW Daniel)

Harvey, Andrew, *Love's Glory: Recreations of Rumi* (Balthazar Books)

Harvey, Andrew, *The Essential Mystics* (Harper Collins)

Judith, Anodea, *Eastern Body, Western Mind* (Celestial Arts)

Joudry, Patricia and Dr M. Pressman, *Twin Souls* (Hazelden)

Johnson, Robert, *The Psychology of Romantic Love* (Penguin Arkana)

Johnson, Robert, *Owning Your Own Shadow* (Harper San Francisco)

Kenyon, Tom and Judith Sion, *The Magdalen Manuscript* (ORB Communications)

Minns, Sue, *Be Your Own Soul Doctor* (Cico)

Monbourquette, John, *How to Befriend Your Shadow* (Darton Longman Todd)

Newton, Dr Michael, *Journey of Souls* (Llewellyn)

Osho, *Trusting Oneself & the Other* (St Martin's Griffin)

Page, Dr Christine, *Spiritual Alchemy* (CW Daniel)

Sagan, Dr Samuel, *Regression* (Clairvision)

St John of the Cross (ed. By Halcyon Backhouse), *The Dark Night of the Soul* (Hodder & Stoughton)

Somers, Barbara with Ian Gordon-Brown, *Journey in Depth* (Archive Publishing)

Todeschi, Kevin J., *Edgar Cayce on Soulmates* (ARE Press)

Vaughan-Lee, Llewellyn, *The Signs of God* (The Golden Sufi Centre)

Vaughan-Lee, Llewellyn, *The Call & the Echo* (Threshold Books)

Soulmates

Walsch, Neale Donald, *Conversations with God* (Hodder Mobius)
Woodman, Marion, *The Ravaged Bridegroom* (Inner City Books)
Woolger, Dr Roger, *Other Lives, Other Selves* (Aquarian)
Young, Louisa, *The Book of the Heart* (Flamingo)
Zukav, Gary, *The Seat of the Soul* (Simon & Schuster)
Zweig, Connie and Jeremiah Abrams, *Meeting the Shadow* (Tarcher Putnam)

useful websites

Astrology Zone: www.astrologyzone.com
College of Psychic Studies: www.psychic-studies.org.uk
Golden Sufi Organisation: www.goldensufi.org
Institute of HeartMath: www.heartmath.org
Spirit of Now: www.peterussel.com